LEGACY
ON THE
ROCKS

The Prehistoric Hunter-Gatherers
of the Matopo Hills, Zimbabwe

ELSPETH PARRY

Illustrated by

JANET DUFF

Oxbow Books
2000

Published by
Oxbow Books
Park End Place, Oxford

© Elspeth Parry, 2000

ISBN 1 84217 010 4

This book is available from

Oxbow Books, Park End Place, Oxford OX1 1HN
Tel: 01865–241249; Fax; 01865–79449
Email: oxbow@oxbowbooks.com

and

The David Brown Book Co.
PO Box 511, Oakville, CT 06779
Tel: (860) 945–9329; Fax: (860) 945–9468
Email: david.brown.bk.co@snet.net

and via our website

www.oxbowbooks.com

Printed in England by
The Short Run Press
Exeter

To
Jessica, Jonathan, Anna, Justin, Alexander
and Max

Contents

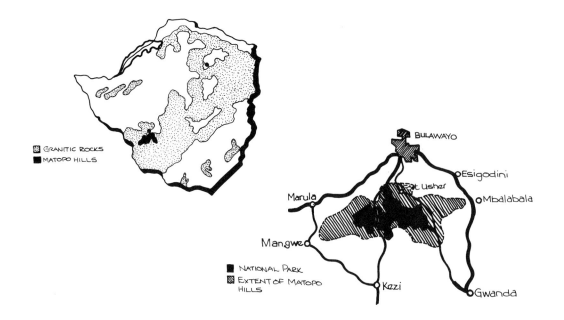

GRANITIC ROCKS
MATOPO HILLS

BULAWAYO
Esigodini
Mbalabala
Marula
Ft Usher
Mangwe
Kezi
Gwanda

NATIONAL PARK
EXTENT OF MATOPO HILLS

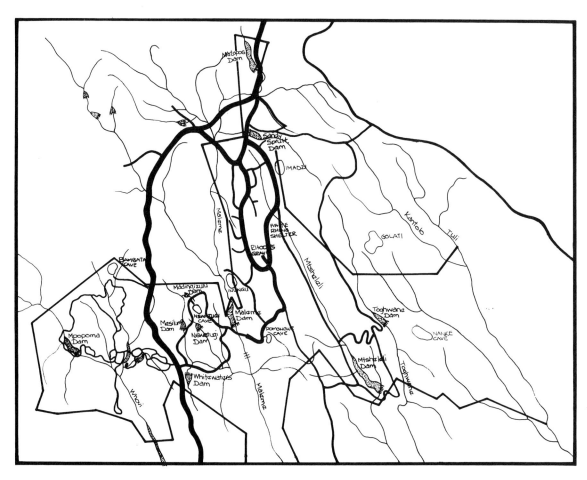

Matobos Dam
Sandy Spruit Dam
Imadzi
Maleme
White Rhino Shelter
Rhodes Grave
Kantol
Tuli
GOLATI
Mtsheleli
Bambata Cave
Madingizulu Dam
Inungu
Malema Dam
Nswatugi Cave
Maleme
Mesilume Cave
Toghwane Dam
Nsewatugi Dam
Pomongwe Cave
Mpopoma Dam
NANKE CAVE
Mtshelell Dam
Whitewaters Dam
Toghwana
Whovi
Maleme

Preface

*"If a man will begin with certainties he shall end in doubts; but if he
will be content to begin with doubts he shall end in certainties."*

FRANCIS BACON

The excitement and wonder experienced in the discovery of ancient
rock paintings is a privilege enjoyed by very few. After several years in
Europe, it was my good fortune to return to Zimbabwe 16 years ago
to come and live on the edge of the magnificent Matopo hills, probably
one of the most densely painted regions in the world. This terrain of
rugged and majestic hills composed of jumbled rocks and great
mountains of granite, interspersed with valleys of trees and tangled,
dense undergrowth, offers perfect protection for the myriad painted
sites. Not easy to find, and lost again with surprising ease.

Long before my arrival a solitary enthusiast had been wandering
the hills, meticulously recording one exciting find after another. It is
to Peter Genge, then Curator of National Monuments, that I owe the
greatest debt of gratitude for his shared knowledge, companionship
and enormous enthusiasm. Peter's knowledge of the Matopo paintings can be surpassed by none, but no one is more circumspect, self
effacing and justifiably protective of the priceless heritage on our
doorstep.

As a whole, in the 18th and early 19th centuries, the first travellers
from Europe showed scant interest in the paintings. More recently,
the civil war in Rhodesia prior to Independence in 1980 made many
painted areas dangerous and inaccessible, contributing to the paucity
of archaeological and ethnological research. Ironically, this has allowed
Zimbabwean rock art to remain largely unseen and therefore protected
from the thoughtless desecration often brought about by human
interest but unfortunately, the present advent of tourism, if uncontrolled, will give rise to vandalism and destruction, as has been
experienced at many sites worldwide. For this reason, illustrations in
this book have no site references. This should not disturb the reader

as all the main caves shown on the map on page vi have attendant custodians and depict a great variety of images.

My years of personally recording rock paintings in the Matopo, and on journeys made to other parts of Zimbabwe, have revealed marked regional differences in content but a sharing of many broadly based concepts in the Bushman art found throughout the country. This book will highlight these regional differences and attempt to give a wider understanding of the painters' way of life, their beliefs and the very structure of a society that could produce such enigmatic, masterful paintings. Unfortunately, systematic and quantitative surveys of the Matopo paintings have not been published and research has been limited to a few enthusiasts. New sites are constantly being discovered and this inevitably makes all records distorted and incomplete.

The following chapters will offer you the known facts and some of the possible interpretations. You, the reader, must reach your own conclusions and in so doing will hopefully acquire a deep respect for a race of extinct people who lived in harmony with their environment and developed a complex culture and artistic tradition. With this appreciation it becomes apparent that the need to preserve the paintings is of utmost importance and this book is written in the hope that all who visit, all who look, appreciate and learn, will care for the environment, value and preserve the paintings, and leave the beauty undisturbed.

My sincere gratitude is extended to the National Parks employees who have been unfailingly helpful and considerate, and to the many commercial farmers and their families for allowing us access to their properties. A very special "thank you" to the late Mrs Peggy Patullo who, almost every Sunday for a year, greeted us from her dairy at 6am before despatching us with her blessing to explore each and every rock on her beautiful farm. I am also indebted to the communal farmers with extensive lands on the outskirts of the National Park who regarded our mission with incredulity but never failed to provide guides and even food and shelter on occasions.

The Matopo, an enchantment of misty mornings, the sun breaking through to cast shadows across the golds and reds of lichen covered rocks. Forgotten still pools, encircled by delicate antelope prints and the paws of the night cats, unseen and moving like wraiths through the sheltering undergrowth. The glorious vistas of rolling hills, the sudden surprise of unexpected animal or bird, new plants and great sheltering trees. Endless unmatched experiences and always the joy of a new painting and the uncanny feeling of the Bushmen's presence. The great writer and good friend, Oliver Ransford, wrote as I feel when he said that in the Matopo, "... one is reminded of Silvio Negro's salutation to his city – *Roma non basta una vita* – for certainly a liftime is not nearly long enough to know these lovely hills completely and intimately." (Ransford, *Bulawayo: Historic Battleground of Rhodesia*, A.A. Balkema, Cape Town, 1968, p. 164)

These years have been a wonderful adventure for me, full of thrilling experiences. In reading this book I hope you might relive some of my excitement and appreciate, as I do, a lost race of great people.

Bushmen or San?

Hunter-gatherers in southern Africa, to this day, have no tribal structure or generic term for themselves. This we may assume applied to our Matopo people 2000 years ago. The Matopans disappeared so long ago that it is debatable how close their way of life resembles the present San of southern Africa, a people exposed to the cultural erosion of differing immigrant races.

Unfortunately, early travellers of the last century saw them as 'primitive' and 'lower than vermin', classifying the different clans collectively as Bushmen, a translation of the Dutch word, *boschjesmans*, implying inferiority. The word Bushman also has irritating sexist overtones. The alternative word 'San' is translated by the Nama Khoikhoi of South Africa to describe poverty-stricken or under-privileged peoples! Hence it is just as pejorative as 'Bushman'.

Neither of these names is appropriate but there is no ideal word, and I will use 'Bushmen' because that is what they have been called in the Matopo since the first paintings were recorded.

In using this word I totally reject any derogatory implications associated with the name Bushman.

Place Names

At Independence in 1980 many place names were changed, and Rhodes's empire became Zimbabwe, as Salisbury became Harare. Throughout the book all names will be used according to the custom of the time.

Methods of Recording

Data forms are used for each site to include: map references, type of site, nature of deposit and artefacts, height above ground level, direction of paintings and site, plus any other pertinent information.

The author and artist never touch the paintings. Using the IFRAO scale, slides and prints are taken and sketches made on site. In the studio, each illustration is traced off the slide with the print and sketch being used for additional reference. The copy is then carefully checked against the original painting. The artist, as a scientific illustrator, is trained to achieve absolute accuracy.

The scale used on all illustrations represents 10cm.

Acknowledgments

I would like to thank Mary Hepenstall for changing my life many years ago, by introducing me to the Matopo paintings; also her sister Mrs Helene Belz whose help and support have made the publication possible. Not many have accompanied me in the field but David Erwee has been an invaluable companion whilst locating and recording sites, Fenton Cotterill in scaling nerve-racking heights and Rob Burrett for reassurance in times of doubt.

My appreciation of Janet Duff's endurance in the field and unswerving dedication to exact replication in the studio knows no bounds. We also shared many diverse and entertaining experiences and had a great time in the making of the book.

Paul Bahn was kind enough to read the manuscript. His active interest has been stimulating and inspiring, I cannot thank him enough.

I am also very grateful to Valerie Lamb of Oxbow Books for coping with the setting of numerous original drawings in the absence of artist and author, both far removed from Oxford.

1

Preservation

Man is the greatest enemy of rock art.
ROBBIE STEEL

Death by Human Assault

In the Matopo rock paintings we have a unique record of a hunter-gatherer society and, by great good fortune, their paintings have largely been left undisturbed although now increasingly vulnerable to the effects of human interest. These are the fragile remains of an early culture, drawn on the rocks more than 2000 years ago and we, the custodians, have this heritage in our care to treasure or destroy.

Natural erosion and weathering must slowly and inexorably cause the paintings to fade and disappear. This process, it is to be hoped, will not be accelerated by human intervention for, unfortunately, every visitor to a painted site can pose a threat.

The need to make a mark or sign a name appears ingrained in the human race and, as early as 1908, the geologist F.P. Mennell writes of graffiti in a Matopo cave.[1]

Touching the paintings accelerates deterioration, especially as many are extremely friable, the paint visibly standing proud from the rock and crumbling to dust at the lightest touch. For this reason the author and artist never touch or trace the images. It can be argued that over the years inestimable damage has been done by researchers in the name of science.[2] Pressing onto an electrostatic material (such as tracing film) with pens and pencils will energize the film, loosening flakes, and can only be regarded as damaging.[3] Fire burns and blackens. A carelessly dropped lighted match becomes an uncontrollable bush fire, the heat causing granitic flaking (exfoliation), and painted surfaces fall away. How often does one find a hearth beneath a group of paintings? The smoke from cooking food drifts across the images leaving a layer of destructive fatty carbon compounds, and yet camp sites are built against rocks, allowing the artwork to be

These are the remains of a large panel being eaten away by the insidious onslaught of lichen. Dashes connect the trees and people as they move through the branches.

incorporated into living areas with no respect for the preservation of antiquity.

Scientific and amateur researchers are now all agreed that painted sites should be protected, where possible, from human abuse. For this very reason the cave of Lascaux, France, was closed to the public with only limited access allowed to researchers. Australian conservators who spent four days monitoring one painted site in the Flinders Ranges found that a quarter of the 91 observed visitors scratched or defaced the rock and it was also shown that tourists tended to touch paintings in small, confined shelters more often than at large open sites.[4] In the Matopo this fact should be borne in mind when taking visitors to small and lesser known sites, and preference should be given to the many well known large and beautifully painted caves in custodial care. These visual extravaganzas delight the eye and illustrate the many facets of the art.

In the Australian National Parks it has been found that extensive tourist promotion of their best rock art sites has encouraged human abuse, and with the ever increasing pressures of tourism, it has been found necessary to install boardwalks to lessen the dust and separate visitors from paintings.[5] Custodial care and caged sites may protect the artwork but metal bars disturb the viewer's appreciation of the paintings, as the joy of this artwork is their setting. Hopefully the necessity for such protective measures will not arise in the Matopo.

To obtain temporary clarity of the images photographers, amongst others, sometimes wet the rock surface which accelerates chemical activity and hastens destruction. Research is being carried out in South Africa on the preservation of rock art and K.I. Meikeljohn of the Pretoria University states: " ... the major concern is that the moisture and thermal regimes of the rock, especially those near the rock surface, are not changed at all. Therefore, wetting the surface for photography may be particularly damaging. Sites with little or no air circulation may even be affected by moisture from the humans who visit the study sites."[6] This reinforces our already stated finding that small sites are more vulnerable to deterioration. Granite rock has the property of being sensitive to moist conditions but resistant when dry. 'As hard as granite' is a saying with little geological verification in this instance. The rock is attacked by the carbon and hydrogen ions in the water, producing oxalic acid which in turn dissolves the iron oxides in the painting pigment, and the image is destroyed.[7]

Until recently, agriculturalists have stored grain in clay bins built against rock walls, these structures sometimes reaching to the painted ceilings and obliterating the images – the builders unknowingly contributing to the destruction of paintings.

Grain bin built against rock paintings

A number of caves have been used by pastoralists over the years to shelter their flocks. The effects of the dust from hooves and feet combined with the rubbing of human and animal bodies on the rock face shows as a reddish stain on the walls, all trace of paintings gone. This practice can still be seen today in the farm areas of the Matopo, and within the rural communities there is an urgent need for environmental education, rewarding the people for custodial care and emphasising the historical importance of painted sites.

In 1963 a National Parks Warden, in a misguided attempt to preserve the Pomongwe cave paintings, covered them with oil. The resulting destruction was further aggravated by dust collecting on the oiled surfaces. Thoughtlessly, at the same time, the cave deposit was levelled, destroying archaeological evidence, and red soil was laid down in an attempt to lessen dust for the visitors. Are the visitors to be protected or the archaeological site?! A careful balance must be struck as the Matopo hills face a rapidly increasing onslaught from tourists and some uninformed tour guides. Many, not content to keep to the approved sites, visit small and unprotected shelters, knowingly or unknowingly causing destruction to the environment of which the paintings are an integral part.

In Zimbabwe the National Museums and Monuments Act 17 of

1972 makes it an indictable offence to alter, damage or remove any National Monument or relic. All rock art sites fall into this category.

We must all treat the hills and rocks as a shrine and a memorial to the Bushmen, to be preserved and not desecrated.

The historical aspect of the hunter-gatherers' life is well illustrated in this small Interpretative Centre at Nswatugi Cave.

Death by Natural Causes

While many paintings are inaccessible to humans, they are still at the mercy of other destructive elements. A multitude of coloured lichens cling to the rocks, presenting glorious contrasting pictures of gold, green, blue and black. These lichens are in an ideal habitat, flourishing in the mists that envelop the hills at certain times of the year; but unfortunately, they too play their part in the destructive process, slowly growing over and obliterating the paintings. Water is retained by the lichens and, as already explained, this activates a damaging process.

Little archaeological research has been carried out in the south-eastern area of the Matopo to determine the degree of Late Stone Age occupation, so we can only assume that the large rivers, the

A termite mound built against a painted wall.

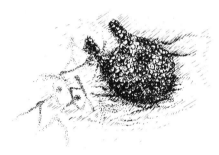

Swallows' nest built against paintings.

abundance of plant and animal life and attractive living areas would have encouraged high levels of human habitation; yet there is a paucity of rock paintings in this area. The explanation may lie in the more turbulent climatic conditions and higher rainfall experienced when the prevailing south-easterly weather impacts on the southern Matopo escarpment, encouraging greater activity in the termite, bird, insect and lichen communities. The natural phenomena of termite mounds, swallow and insect nests, built over the centuries, against cave walls and covering the paintings may explain the total absence of images in many obviously suitable sites. Vast termite mounds cling to the rock faces, creeping up the walls to meet generations of swallows' nests, nature's destructive fingers plucking at the vulnerable paintings.

Habitually the dassie, a prolific small mammal, urinates on rocky middens, the liquid seeping over the surface and creating an organic, mineral glaze which obscures the art. The droppings of birds nesting on rocky outcrops may also cover and obliterate paintings.

Some surfaces, possibly due to the structure of the granite, seem more prone to exfoliation than others. This is a process brought about by successive heating and cooling of the granite and the eventual splitting away of rocky slivers large and small, carrying the painted images with them. The traditional doctors, N'angas, still utilise specific parts of an image, ground to a fine powder and administered as a powerful medicine with magical potency, and this damaging process of chipping and pecking at the granite surface can be mistaken for exfoliation (see page 7).

A Lethal Combination

Natural weathering inevitably plays a part in the destruction of rock paintings, but human interference can cause rapid and catastrophic damage within a very short period of time. In South Africa during this century dramatic deterioration has taken place at rock art sites, but unfortunately it is only in recent years that protective measures have been attempted. Rock art researcher and conservationist, J. Loubser, made the alarming observation that, "... a few years of human visitation can cause more damage to rock paintings than centuries of natural weathering."[8]

Eventually the paintings will disappear, but let us not hasten the

The rhino horns have been chipped off, presumably by local N'angas to use as medicine. The main scene is touched with unreality in sharp contrast to the three realistic women above. These figures resemble the rhino and buck-headed snake in Nswatugi Cave (p. 104). The two sites are approximately 10 km apart. Unusually a lizard appears.

Bushmen ethnology speaks of the healer throwing ropes to the sky with which to climb during out of body travel, but since there is no recorded oral history in the Matopo, this myth can only be a surmise.

process. The eminent art critic and historian, Herbert Read, warns us not to underestimate the true value of art for, "Art is a mode of knowledge, and the world of art is a system of knowledge as valuable to man as the world of philosophy or the world of science. Indeed, it is only when we have clearly recognised art as a mode of knowledge, parallel to and distinct from other modes by which man arrives at an understanding of his environment, that we can begin to appreciate its significance in the history of mankind."[9] Rock art is a finite, fragile and irreplaceable resource.

World-wide tourism has become a major source of income and Zimbabwe is no exception; but our environment must be protected, our paintings preserved. It is our responsibility to allow future generations the opportunity to appreciate the great artistic talent and fascinating painted story of the Bushmen's life.

2

Dating

"History, the story of men and their achievements, is not intelligible until we realise that it is a part of prehistory – and of the natural history – of Man. And unless our history is intelligible to us not much else will be."

ALAN HOUGHTON BRODRICK

How about a date?

Every visitor asks the same two questions of the paintings, "what does this mean?" and "how old are they?" Both age and interpretation have an equal fascination for scientists and laymen but there are no easy answers. Here we will address the problem of dating and, later in the book, explore the convoluted avenues of interpretation.

The early researchers claimed to recognise stylistic sequences in the art, this being the accepted method of placing the paintings in historical time. In the Matopo there were thought to be three to four sequences in styles, the first represented by human and animal silhouettes and a second period characterised by outline drawings. In phase three the images were of considerable size and the human figures were assumed

Perfect artistry in the outline shape of the lion, no longer seen in the Matopo.

to depict different cultures. Cooke went on to describe the fourth and final stage as an "artistic explosion" for which "a more complex palette was used into which white had been introduced for the first time" and he said, "Landscape compositions showing trees and rocks also appear."[1]

This controversial method has still been used quite recently in Europe. Today, Robert Bednarik, the rock art specialist, queries that, "If the dating rests solely on stylistic observations, what precisely are these, how does one express them in an empirical, quantifiable or repeatable form, and how does one test them? To give an example: we hear sometimes about "twisted perspective" being a stylistic marker. Since it occurs in many art traditions of the world, how can it be a dating criterion?"[2]

This method of dating was discarded some time ago in Southern Africa when archaeologists began to use the radiocarbon dating technique based on a measurable level of radiocarbon in dead animal and plant tissue. This method yields reliable ages back to about 50 000 BP (before the present). The atmospheric concentration of radiocarbon is incorporated into all living things through carbon dioxide. This is absorbed by plants during photosynthesis, which are then eaten by herbivorous animals and they in turn are eaten by carnivores (see Diagram on this page). Carbon dioxide absorption only ceases on death when the carbon content starts to decline. The age of dead plant or animal tissue is calculated by measuring the amount of radiocarbon remaining and knowing the decay rate, but archaeologists were assuming that the age of the identifiable radiocarbon in the paint and the age of the image were identical. This assumption cannot be made as material of differing ages may have been used in the paint preparation and the image may have been overpainted or embellished at a later stage. The possibility then arises of obtaining two differing dates from one image.

It is not necessary to enter here into the complexity of scientific detail, but it is important to realise that radiocarbon dating is a

Carbon-14
↓
Carbon Dioxide
↓

↓

↓

↓

Radiocarbon (^{14}C) is continually being formed in the atmosphere. It is incorporated into all living things through carbon dioxide.

↓

Plants absorb carbon dioxide during photosynthesis. When the plant dies, the intake of radiocarbon ceases.

↓

Charcoal is made from the plant.

↓

Charcoal is used in the preparation of paint.

Carbon-14
↓   →
Carbon Dioxide

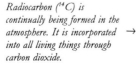

Radiocarbon (^{14}C) is continually being formed in the atmosphere. It is incorporated into all living things through carbon dioxide. → *Plants absorb carbon dioxide during photosynthesis.* → *Animals eat leaves and absorb ^{14}C.* → *When the animal dies, the intake of radiocarbon ceases.* → *The bones of animals are later dug up by archaeologists.*

complicated process and the outcome affected by many variable factors such as climate, vegetation and other unknown forces. Bacteria, algae and fungi will also appear in the paint and will inevitably affect the outcome. Hardwood trees in Zimbabwe remain standing for many years after death when radiocarbon uptake ceases so dating old wood charcoal may not date the act of applying charcoal as a paint. Also, old charcoal could have lain in sheltered secluded caves for hundreds of years.

For this method of dating it is necessary to know the initial concentration of carbon and the decay rate of the sample. Robert Bednarik, arguing against the possibility of accurate dating by this method, feels that, "Contrary to theoretical expectations and popular archaeological belief, there is not a 68,26% certainty that the true age of a sample would fall within the tolerances stated."[3]

Initially, this method was applied to archaeological finds and the paintings were forgotten as archaeologists plunged into this exciting scientific method, mistakenly assuming that this would reveal all one wanted to know of prehistory. However, this was not to be.

Artefacts are the most visible records of past societies and in the continuous search for reliable dating techniques archaeologists have regarded humans' tools as markers in history, to delineate the differing ages into which progress through time could be classified. This useful archaeological formalisation has been used in the dating of painted rock spalls found during excavation of assemblages of early artefacts. Despite the proximity to a datable artefact, the accuracy of the dating is doubtful, especially in the Matopo where granite flakes away at unpredictable rates and can exfoliate at random, meaning that the painted fragment may have fallen hundreds of years after the painting was executed to lie with much younger artefacts. This renders the method vague and unreliable and only some of what is depicted in rock art confirms the information found on excavation.

Only in very recent years has it been discovered that organic materials such as blood, oxalate, fossilised micro-organisms and plant fibre within the paint, can be isolated and used in a sophisticated radiocarbon dating technique known as Accelerator Mass Spectrometry Radiocarbon Dating (AMS). This is a method that utilises an accelerator mass spectrometer to determine the actual numbers of 14C atoms present in a sample rather than the relatively small numbers of 14C atoms that decay radioactively during the measurement time of the conventional method. Samples needed are far smaller using AMS, as demonstrated by the necessity for 10 to 25 g of wood for the conventional method as opposed to 50 to 100mg for AMS. Another advantage is that the AMS method takes hours whereas the old

Hand axe: These tools of various sizes were probably used in dismembering and skinning an animal

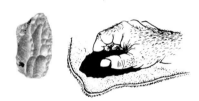

Side scraper: Used to dress hides.

Borer: Was probably used as an awl to punch holes in animal skins.

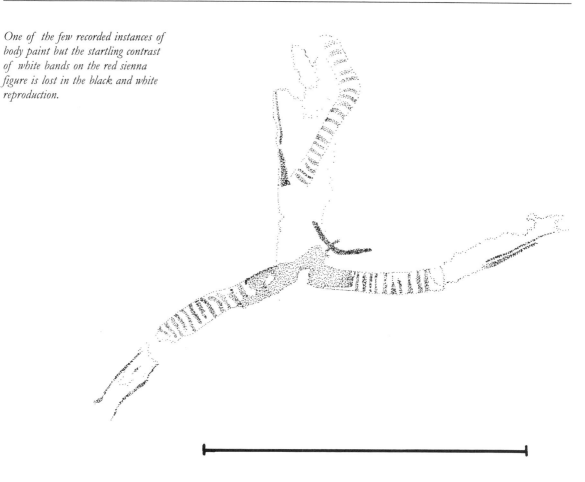

One of the few recorded instances of body paint but the startling contrast of white bands on the red sienna figure is lost in the black and white reproduction.

radiocarbon technique takes days. This method also allows dating of textiles and artefacts without destruction of the artefact. Paint removal is minimised in the interests of preservation. Unfortunately, a fundamental obstacle is the enormous amount of expertise needed and consequently the expense involved.

The Matopo paintings have not yet been dated using the AMS method, but regardless of age their historical value is of immeasurable importance and expands our knowledge of past cultures.

Until this accurate method of dating can be applied it is of vital importance that the words of Alan Watchman, the rock art dating specialist, are heeded and, "... under no circumstances whatsoever should the engraved rock surfaces be treated with any organic or inorganic carbon-bearing substance, including the materials for making casts, the production of rubbings, spraying to remove lichen, using soaps or other chemicals to clean chalk or other graffiti until after samples for AMS ^{14}C dating have been removed. Doing so will contaminate the rock surface and lead to false ages for the surface accretions."[4]

At present, in order to date the art, we rely on the more traditional archaeological, ethnological and possibly stylistic techniques from which it would seem that this artistic tradition stretches back to at least 13 000 years BP, but subsequent to 2 200 BP and by 1 500 BP the hunter-gatherers of the Matopo had disappeared. Over the years much ancient art will have vanished and it would seem that we are now looking at the remnants of painting done in the later Stone Age.[5]

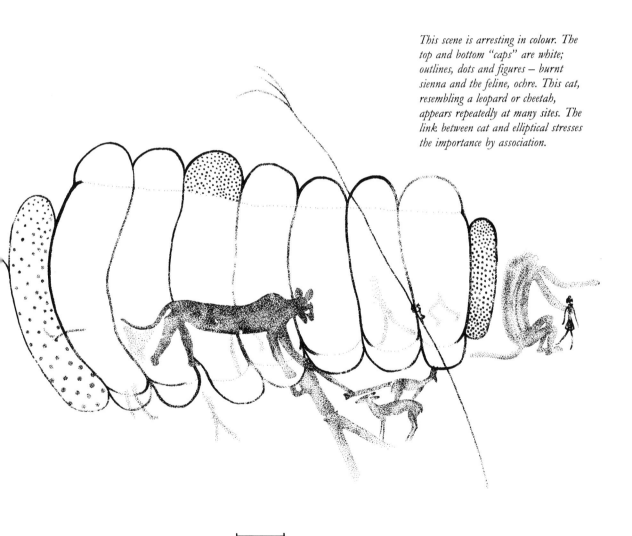

This scene is arresting in colour. The top and bottom "caps" are white; outlines, dots and figures — burnt sienna and the feline, ochre. This cat, resembling a leopard or cheetah, appears repeatedly at many sites. The link between cat and elliptical stresses the importance by association.

3

And in the Beginning ...

"What you see and hear now, are the echoes of the joys and sorrows through the centuries which come from the hearts of a people that wander over the face of the earth. You, a product of tarmac-road civilisation, can never be a part of it. You can only be a spectator." (As said by Xameb, a Bushman, to the author P.J. Schoeman)

The Matopo hills hold a strange and compelling fascination for us all. There is within these hills a strong spiritual attraction that appeals to people from all over the world. This is a place of enchantment that many years ago sheltered and sustained a great race of people. These hunter-gatherers, who throughout history have been branded as primitive, their way of life condemned, their great talents for environmental adaptability and artistic genius unrecognised, are now gone. All that remains are their enigmatic paintings – a fading legacy upon the rocks.

When and where did this begin? It was three million years ago here in Africa, the 'cradle of humankind', that *Homo sapiens* evolved from their primate ancestors and eventually became the Bushmen of our story.

There is no escaping the reality that the Bushmen are us! Certainly, as J.S. Krüger points out, "The biology, sociology and psychology of our species were formed during the hunter-gatherer period, a relatively long one in terms of human development."[1] and it is an astonishing fact that for 99% of humans' time on earth, we have been hunter-gatherers! The image of them as intellectually degraded and backward must be discarded. A delightful and pertinent analogy by the anthropologist Melvin Konner points out that, "Inasmuch as genetic change in the mere ten thousand years since the advent of agriculture has probably been trivial, the argument goes, we are in essence hunter-gatherers transplanted out of skins and huts into three-piece suits and high-rise condominiums."[2]

The historical written records of central Africa are sparse, vague and inexact. As far back as the eleventh century Arab traders on the east coast of Africa described Khoisan people, speaking a click language, as the "Wak-Wak" and in 1498, the Portuguese in Sofala made reference to "Abutwa - the land of the small people"[3] which may possibly have been the hinterland of today's Zimbabwe, but this can only have been the vestigial remains of our race of painters.

Much, if not all, of the rock art to be seen today in the Matopo was

Diagramatic time scale.

(BC) ASIA/MID EAST	EUROPE	AFRICA
2500– First civilization in Indus Valley. First Indian writing. Towns built on grid system & drainage & central heating used in India. Rice cultivation reaches Southeast Asia from southern China. 1900- First Chinese script and calendar.	**2000–** Stonehenge is built.	**2500–** Beginning of hieroglyphic writing in Egypt. First Sub-Saharan pastoralists appear in Kenya & Tanzania. **1300–600–** Saharan Bronze Age. **1250–** Moses leads Hebrews out of Egypt.
1000– Hebrew alphabet is developed	**1000–** Greeks adopt Phoenician alphabet. **776–** First Olympic Games. **753–** Foundation of Rome.	**1000–** King Solomon's temple is built. **650–** Iron is first used in Egypt.
450– Coinage begins to be minted by Phoenicians.	**447–** Parthenon is built. **335–** First coinage minted in Rome.	**360–** First coinage struck in Egypt.
300– Building begins on the Great Wall of China		**0–200AD–** Herding & mixed farming begins in Southern Africa.

done by the Late Stone Age hunter-gatherers. This was the great age of painting but, despite the high density of painted sites, much has been lost and sometimes the only remaining evidence is painted spalls (splintered rock) buried deep in cave deposits. Peter Garlake, in his most recent publication, *The Hunter's Vision*, emphasises the fact that the rock paintings "... are so old that the societies that created them disappeared entirely so long ago that they are absent not just from the region's short recorded history but, except in the most shadowy and fragmentary form, from folk memory as well."[4]

These Stone Age people fashioned primitive tools from many types of stone until in the Late Stone Age, 28 000 years ago, human hands produced the sophistication of bone needles, microlith arrow heads, fine scrapers for leather preparation, eggshell beads and many other precursors of our modern day technology. Hunter-gatherers were spread throughout southern Africa and in the Matopo they occupied

The clarity of these hunters on the rock is quite astonishing, yet the heads have disappeared. The hook head on the right would indicate that the face was painted white, the fugitive colour, and the possibility remains that the heads to the left were also white.

Artefacts found on excavation at Bambata Cave: discoidal scraper, borer, eggshell beads, and incised ostrich eggshell.

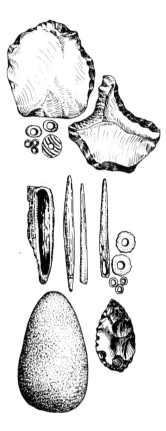

Artefacts found on excavation at Nswatugi Cave: point sharpener, bone point, matting needle, eyed needle, eggshell beads, a heavy-duty stone implement (hammerstone) and a point.

caves and shelters, leaving behind artefacts from which we can attempt a reconstruction of their life and culture.

Humankind has been in Africa for many thousands of years, existing as hunter-gatherers, struggling to survive climatic variations and adapting to environmental change, relying on an evolving knowledge of wood and stone implements to improve his chances of survival. Agriculture and domestic animals were unknown but society was developing a technological sophistication and during this time we see the invention of the bow and arrow, so often depicted in prehistoric paintings, and the discovery of poison that markedly increased the effectiveness of hunting.

Agriculture and Change

10 000 years ago in Europe, Asia and north Africa, the emergence of agriculture signalled a profound change in the history of humankind and revolutionised the hunter-gatherers' life style. People would no longer roam the land gathering wild plants, trapping and hunting wild animals. Grains would be cultivated, animals herded and penned. The new agriculturalists in the northern hemisphere learned to make clay pots and weave baskets, and gradually their knowledge spread. Migration southwards through Africa was slow and hazardous as there were many obstacles to overcome but, possibly due to population pressures and land hunger, the herders crossed the Sahara desert which had become increasingly drier and inhospitable, presenting a massive but not impossible obstacle. Further south, great forest areas formed impenetrable barriers. Wide rivers and malarial swamps hampered movement and discouraged settlement. Despite all this, migratory groups of people together with their domestic stock moved down the east and west coasts and appeared in Central Africa approximately 2000 years ago. Walker estimates that, " At about 2150 BP, domestic animals, almost certainly including at least sheep, were introduced into the economy [in the Matopo]. The introduction of stock into the area coincided with the first appearance of pottery. The pottery is a sophisticated ware ... [and] has affinities with the subsequent Iron Age traditions, and so is regarded as imported and traded from early immigrant herders."[5]

The evidence for interaction between the Bushmen and the herders within Zimbabwe is very limited. This sparse evidence is due to the paucity of archaeological work in this area, and a gap remains between east and central Africa and southern Africa. The paintings in the Matopo show no domestic stock as is found south of the Limpopo

Pottery and pot sherds. The heavily incised sherd is Bambata ware.

river valley and to a lesser extent north in Mashonaland. This poses an ethnological puzzle. What caused the Matopan society to disappear, leaving no evidence in the paintings of integration with the immigrant herders? The probabilities are many. Firstly: enforced isolation; secondly: assimilation or elimination by the immigrant peoples; and thirdly: disease, or environmental degradation due to overpopulation. Let us investigate the feasibility of these options.

It could be surmised that the migrants dominated the surrounding flatlands driving the hunter-gatherers into the fastness of the hills until pressure of numbers and environmental collapse brought about their end. A proud people, did they choose to remain isolated in order to retain their cultural identity? This would seem unlikely as hunter-gatherers in historic time have assimilated with the pastoralists in southern Africa, experiencing an amicable interchange of cultural traditions and establishing a relatively peaceful co-existence. It was not until the dominant European settlers staked their claims on the previously communal land and indigenous animals that aggressive clashes occurred which eventually gravely decimated the Bushmen.

It has been found in the Kalahari that the hunter-gatherers' diet and life-style protected them from disease, but over-population could have precipitated a catastrophic situation. Present day hunter-gatherers, as in the Kalahari, are strongly motivated to limit population but the extremely favourable living conditions in the Matopo may have encouraged a sense of 'false security'. If overpopulation occurred, environmental degradation would most certainly have ensued, forcing the people out of the hills. The absence of domestic animals in the paintings, the mark of the immigrant people, is a strong indication that the Matopo was a depopulated landscape when the herders arrived.

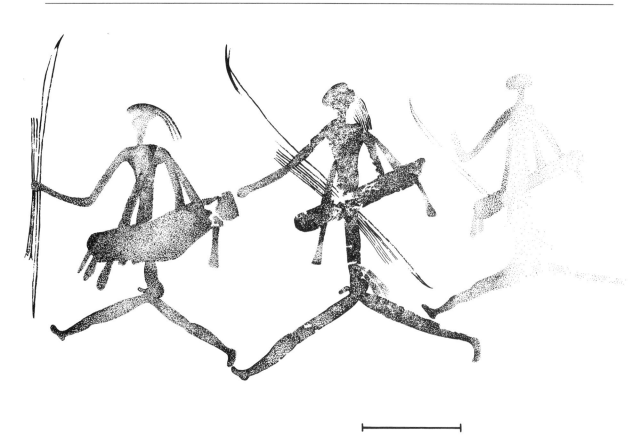

These hunters with their bird-like head-dresses run or almost fly across the rocks. Eight hurrying figures but only these two so clear, the remnants on a long wall of many faded images.

Had the Bushmen moved to the north and south? The paintings to the north of the Matopo are of startling clarity and, although undated, appear younger, and images of fat-tailed sheep are occasionally seen. To the south, in the Limpopo valley, the images, painted on sandstone, a friable and easily degrading rock, are markedly different (see page 28). Longevity of these paintings is precluded by the nature of the rock, therefore, a recent age for the paintings must be postulated, possibly within the last 500 years. Here we can speculate that sub-cultures had arisen in the last 2 000 years and the images of fat-tailed sheep point to assimilation by the immigrants. The Matopo environment was capable of sustaining the Bushmens' livelihood throughout the year, assuming a carefully regulated population but, for whatever reason, painting seems to have ceased abruptly approximately 1500 years ago[6] and an historic epoch was concluded. We may never know for certain whether disease, over-population, environmental degradation, assimilation or emigration left the hills deserted. This enigma, in a land-locked island of hills, can be likened to Jared Diamond's description of marine islands that through history have left us with one of, "... the most tantalising mysteries of archaeology ... the unexplained disappearances of human populations isolated on islands."[7]

And now ...

Moving forward rapidly into the present and most recent past, the field of study is large but researchers few. The earliest known publication in Zimbabwe to mention rock art was by the archaeologist, J. Theodore Bent, who made sketches of some paintings in Mutoko, Mashonaland, in 1891.[8] While admiring the ability of the artists he dismisses the content as of little importance!

Richard Hall, the first Curator of Great Zimbabwe Ruins, took an interest in the paintings and described many sites, including 27 small and insignificant shelters within the Matopo.[9] His vivid imagination produced some fanciful interpretations, for instance, he saw the recurring elliptical images as representations of the Victoria Falls! Taking into account the prevailing attitudes of the time, the lack of ethnographic interest or appreciation of the Bushmen's abilities is hardly surprising, but fortunately a less bigoted and more enlightened approach was on the way.

A museum had been established in Bulawayo in 1902 and successive Curators took a varying degree of interest in the Matopo paintings. It was not until 1935 when Neville Jones, a missionary with an enthusiasm for archaeology and geology, was appointed to the museum as Keeper of Prehistory, that any serious attention was paid to the wealth of rock art on their doorstep. He had already completed careful archaeological excavations in the Matopo and in 1926 had published *The Stone Age in Rhodesia*. Writing at the end of this book his sense of the enormity of the task upon which he had embarked is very evident and he says ruefully, "How little I have really said. Everywhere we turn we seem hemmed in by a cloud of impenetrable darkness, in which we grope, if haply we may be able to shed some light on the history of the forgotten peoples of this great land. The importance of endeavouring to gather up every thread of evidence and of following up every clue can hardly be over emphasised."[10]

His name was known far beyond the borders of Rhodesia, and the Royal Anthropological Institute of London conferred upon him the rare honour of Honorary Life Membership. A fearless Christian and the father of Rhodesian pre-history, his Matabele friends gave him the honourable name of Mhlagazanhlansi – 'he who blows on the embers and stirs the fire'. By his application to scientific detail and archae-

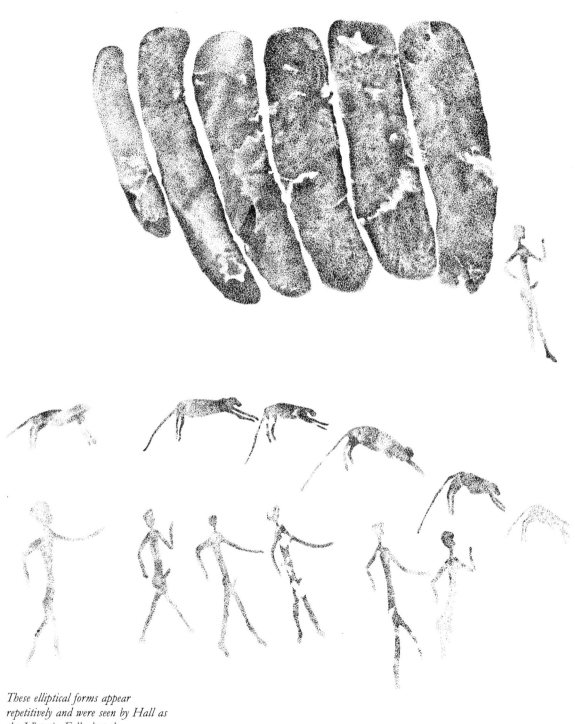

*These elliptical forms appear
repetitively and were seen by Hall as
the Victoria Falls, but they are
variously interpreted as granite rocks,
beehives or centres of potency. The
line of Mongoose is unusual.*

ological awareness, although he may not have known it, Neville Jones gave Zimbabwean rock art a base on which to build a framework of scientific analysis.

One of our earliest and perhaps most enthusiastic amateur 'collectors' of rock art, Lionel Cripps, came to Rhodesia in 1890. He was appointed as a Commissioner to the newly convened "Monuments and Relics Commission" in 1936. Prior to this, during his term of office and after retiring, he travelled throughout the country, including the Matopo, finding and tracing hundreds of paintings, filling eleven large volumes which are now housed at the Museum of Human Sciences, Harare. Cripps was the first to appreciate that this was not decorative art, realising that "primitive people are purposeful in a serious way and their undertakings are carried out in that spirit and not merely as a way of passing the time."[11]

This clarity of vision was not emulated by one Samuel Impey, a Cape Town doctor with an interest in rock art. Having published a book in 1926 on southern African paintings,[12] denigrating the Bushmen

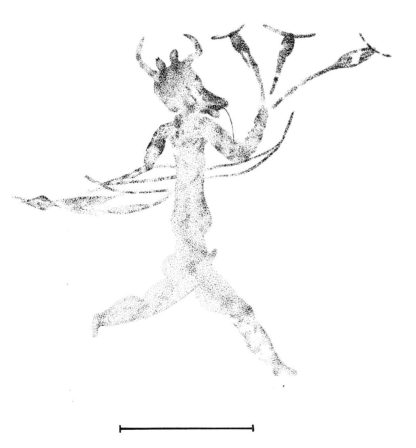

Some detail was missed when Neville Jones copied this painting in the 1930s for the cover of his book The Prehistory of Southern Rhodesia. *The hunter is either therianthropic or masked. This is a very vulnerable site used by picnickers.*

Frobenius saw wedge shaped figures such as this, as indicating a greater depth of meaning than the paintings had previously been credited with (see Heritage of Zimbabwe, No. 12, p. 9). *The small snake on p. 110 appears to the right, and these are the only two remaining clear images on a wall of degraded paintings.*

and suggesting a Mediterranean influence, he subsequently appeared in Rhodesia to expand on these ideas. Undeterred by his unpopular concepts, Impey presented a paper at the South African Association for the Advancement of Science in Salisbury (Harare) in July 1927. Havoc ensued but his wild theories were fortunately discounted by other more informed members of the Conference.

During the 1920s, international archaeologists and ethnographers were attracted to southern Africa's artistic wealth. Miles Burkitt, a leading prehistorian at the time, came out from Cambridge and toured Rhodesia, visiting a few major sites but only one in the Matopo. He saw the paintings from the archaeologists' point of view and with no ethnological interests was unable to perceive any hidden meanings or cultural interpretations within the paintings. The drawings represented to him a picture of the Bushmen's daily life.

By contrast, the ethnographer Leo Frobenius, Founder and President of the Institute of Cultural Morphology at Frankfurt-on-Main, applied himself more diligently. Here was a giant among the early scientists. Following hard on the heels of Burkitt, he assessed the hidden depths and meanings of the artwork with a perception and appreciation unlike any of his predecessors. Between 1904 and 1932, he led ten scientific expeditions to Africa and Asia, and during the time in southern Africa he and his researchers made over 400 copies of paintings in Rhodesia, including the Matopo. Subsequently, Frobenius produced a classic rock art research publication entitled: *Madsimu Dsangara – The Pictures of the Forgotten Ones.*[13] His stamina and dedication seem to have been inexhaustible and inbetween his various commitments he managed to produce no less than 60 books! Emotionally gripped by his subject, he hoped to take his reader to the heart of the hunter-gatherers' culture and infect one with his enthusiasm and understanding. Today we must admire the depth of his vision, his appreciation of the possible symbolic meanings in the artwork leading to shamanistic ritual transformations. This intuitive approach was scorned at the time and it was not until recent years that a full appreciation has been felt for a researcher so far ahead of his time.

In 1929, a Frenchman, the Abbé Henri Breuil, a friend and mentor of Miles Burkitt, now appeared in Rhodesia and briefly visited the Matopo, adding his theories to the somewhat heated discussions! Having done extensive research in Namibia, his conviction that Mediterranean influence dominated those rock paintings spilled over into his interpretation of the Rhodesian art. This was a sorry reflection of the accepted dogma at that time, promoting Europe's superiority in this field and the inability to credit the so-called "primitive" tribes with aptitude and skills. Despite numerous visits to Rhodesia he never

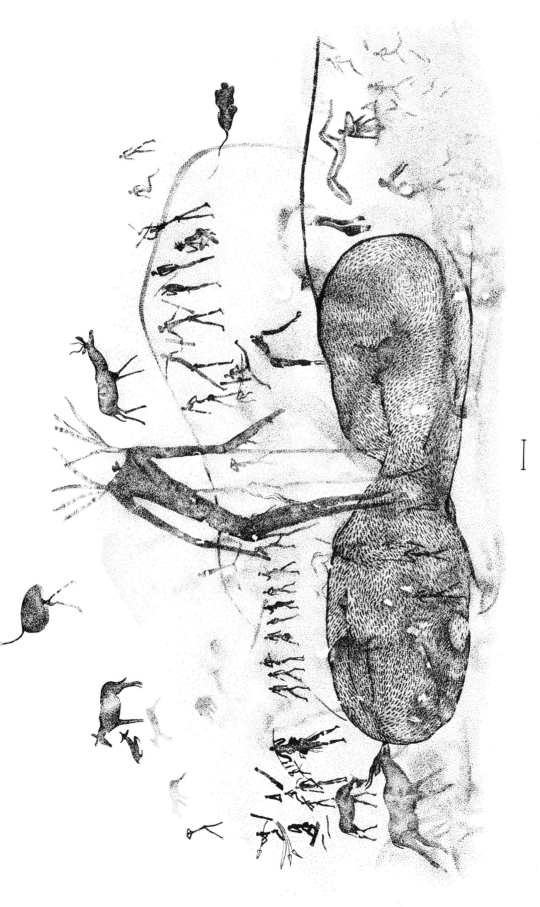

An association of images that has fascinated researchers and copyists, including Frobenius, since Nanke Cave was first visited and recorded, but few have portrayed the detail you see here. The broken dashes are drawn to strict design contained within the outer continuous line which then moves away to connect, touch and encompass other images. The large antelope to the left, reaching out to touch the 'pond', has the 'jizz' of the Nyala, now only found sporadically in the Lowveld of Zimbabwe.

changed his mind and one can only agree with Peter Garlake's opinion that, "Breuil's work in Rhodesia is a sad and cautionary tale of the results of fame, of decades of unchallenged authority leading to dogmatic assertions, derived from cursory examinations, inaccurate copying, complete lack of systematic comparative studies and the isolation of tendentiously selected items from their contexts."[14]

A woman now emerges to hold the limelight for many years. Elizabeth Goodall was a member of the Frobenius Afrika Expedition, travelling as an assistant to Leo Frobenius; and as a pupil of his she remained loyal to his theories and convictions throughout her life. In 1931 she returned to Rhodesia and married, remaining to study rock art and becoming Honorary Keeper of Rock Paintings at the Queen Victoria Museum in Salisbury. She was essentially an artist and appreciated the aesthetic and creative qualities in the art. Her watercolours captured the imaginative feel and mastery of the paintings although sometimes, it must be said, she used some degree of artistic license!

No history of Zimbabwean rock art research would be complete without acknowledging the great achievements of Cran Cooke. Cranmer K. Cooke emigrated from Britain to Rhodesia in 1929 and, as a policeman on mounted patrols in the north of the country, he came upon many painted sites, further stimulating an existing interest

These Nswatugi Cave duiker appear in The Rock Art of Central Africa, *p. 125, and were copied by Cran Cooke. The original is in the possession of the author. He used the old stylistic method to date them and classifies the paintings as Style four.*

in archaeology. On his settling in Bulawayo, this became a serious pastime and in 1952 he was appointed Secretary to the Historical Monuments Commission of Southern Rhodesia which eventually amalgamated with the National Museums in 1972. Cooke, with his infectious enthusiasm, operated with a small and dedicated staff, and after 30 years service in various capacities he retired in 1987 at the age of 81! Overwhelmingly industrious and a prolific writer, his work put the Rhodesian paintings on the world archaeological map. In 1959, he collaborated with Elizabeth Goodall and the archaeologist Desmond Clark in producing a comprehensive book on the *Prehistoric Rock Art of the Federation of Rhodesia and Nyasaland*.[15]

Cran, as he was affectionately called, applied a practical approach to the art and wrote that, "The whole of the realistic art appears to have been based on the simple principle that some people like to paint and have the ability to do so, whilst others can admire and of course criticize".[16] Yet he glimpsed that there might be more to this art form than pure decoration when he wrote in the same book, "... there are outcrops of painting, usually away from the main painted shelters, which do not appear to conform with the accepted method in drawing and sometimes, but more rarely, in the basic technique. In these isolated paintings the artist's powers of expression often take unusual forms; some have the gay abandon of the expressionist, whilst others can only be referred to as caricatures".[17] Although himself an artist, Cran allowed for no hidden meanings or obscure cultural explanations. His realistic interpretations have been dismissed by present day researchers but this in no way discredits one of Zimbabwe's most noteworthy archaeologists.

This was not the age of the art historian but there were ethnographers who were to follow with new and alternative interpretations for the great parade of drawings spread lavishly across the rocks.

To bring us up to date, the recent and innovative approach by Peter Garlake brings a refreshing, if controversial analysis to the rock paintings of Zimbabwe. Garlake has worked as an archaeologist in Africa for 30 years and his publications offer fascinating interpretation of many drawings unique to Zimbabwe.

From the turn of the century, books have been published on many aspects of southern African rock art, describing the paintings and offering varying interpretations. These differences are the product of each author's academic and social circumstances.

There is strong evidence in Zimbabwe that imagery, highlighting cultural differences, is tied to geographical areas and this agrees with J.S. Kruger's findings that, " the many fluid Bushmen groups, adapted and responded to a great variety of environmental conditions over a

This style of drawing may have given the early researcher, Cran Cooke, the idea that they were caricatures. A series of similar images occur 5–8 km to the west, but are not illustrated in the book. The small head and expanded body are now interpreted as synonymous with the trance experience.

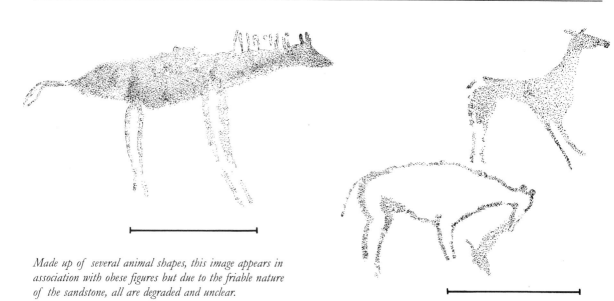

Made up of several animal shapes, this image appears in association with obese figures but due to the friable nature of the sandstone, all are degraded and unclear.

This unusual image from the low veld had also been seen in South Africa but not in the Matopo.

This zoomorphic figure, seen in the low veld, is described in the journal, Fragile Icons, *p. 10, as possibly representing a feline shaman transformation.*

Rising like wraiths or ghostly spirits, these shapes are commonly found on the sandstone of the low veld region in Zimbabwe, but not seen by the author in the Matopo.

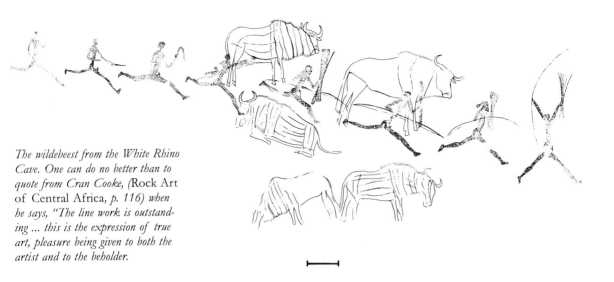

The wildebeest from the White Rhino Cave. One can do no better than to quote from Cran Cooke, (Rock Art of Central Africa, p. 116) when he says, "The line work is outstanding ... this is the expression of true art, pleasure being given to both the artist and to the beholder.

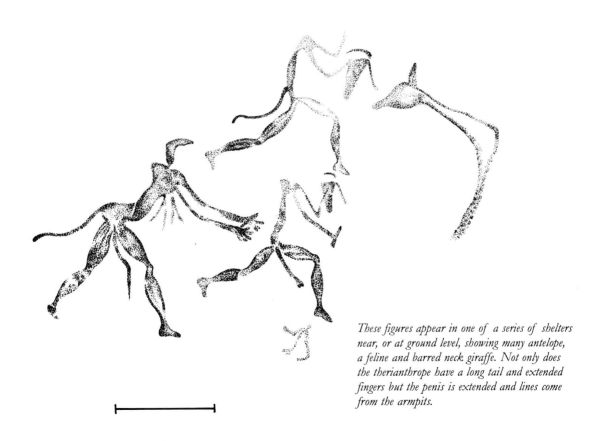

These figures appear in one of a series of shelters near, or at ground level, showing many antelope, a feline and barred neck giraffe. Not only does the therianthrope have a long tail and extended fingers but the penis is extended and lines come from the armpits.

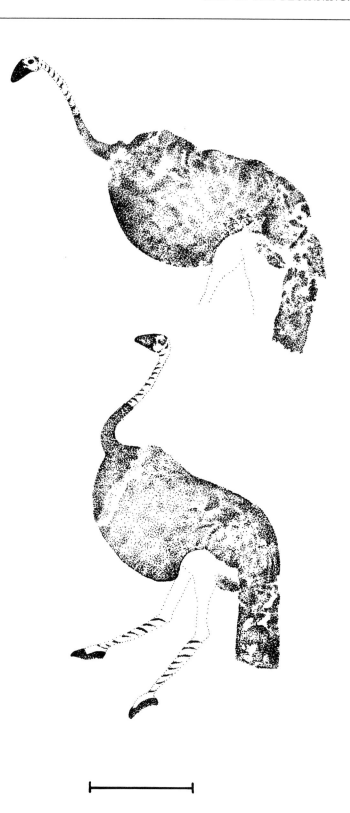

This is a bird still seen in the Matopo, reintroduced when the Park was created, and the enquiring nature of the ostrich is beautifully portrayed in the position of the head.

long period and in the process developed a wide range of cultural forms".[18] The painted sandstone shelters of the Limpopo river valley, to the south of the Matopo, show marked differences in imagery. Floating 'Y' shaped figures, geometric designs and hand prints separate this art from that seen in the Matopo. Obese and distended figures are virtually confined to Mashonaland. These distorted human images appear very infrequently in the Matopo. The part-bird, part-man figures and animal-human forms known as "therianthropes" occur frequently in the Matopo, and on this point I take issue with Peter Garlake who states, "there is extremely little in the Zimbabwe paintings that could be called 'therianthropic'".[19] Comparative imagery between these different areas is of importance in the interpretation of Zimbabwean rock art if we are to understand the cultural differences of the complex societies that created them.

Look deeply and carefully into the paintings. This is not just decorative art. These drawings are as words in a book. As we unravel the woven skeins of meaning in every painting, creating a complex picture of the realities and unrealities of the Bushmen way of life, we will marvel not only at their artistic merit but also at the intricacies of a vanished culture, always remembering, as archaeologist John Kinahan points out, that "In view of the great complexity of recent hunter gatherer history, and the often ambiguous nature of the archaeological record, it seems to me unwise to dismiss out of hand an explanation that is at least as well supported as any other."[20]

4

The Matopo

"The Matopo hills, that extraordinary, fascinating granite country where huge boulders are piled on other boulders as if giants of long ago had been playing with bricks upon a giant nursery floor, and, growing tired, petulantly left them in glorious confusion."

MILES BURKITT

The Matopo, a majestic landscape of great granite domes and tumbled rock interspersed with wooded valleys and deep gorges, has captured the imaginations of early travellers and present day visitors, filled them with awe and inspired them to return time and time again. The hills have a magic of their own. An early visitor to the Matopo said: "No pen picture can do justice to the riotous grandeur of this extraordinary range, which nature has constructed in one of her most freakish moods."[1] Although not high, these hills for the uninitiated can be intimidating and confusing. To even the most intrepid explorer – deceiving, wild and impenetrable.

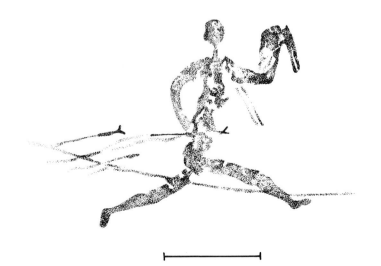

The degraded nature of this image makes identification of the object in the left hand impossible. The long line between the legs of the figure continues for 1.5m to the left connecting with the 'fish pond' on p. 25.

Matopo landscape.

Through the years some confusion has arisen over the correct name for the area, now popularly known as 'the Matopos'; however, this is incorrect as the word Matopo, which is used in this book, is already in the plural. The name would seem to be a corruption of 'Matombo' the Kalanga word for hills, and an alternative corruption, Matobo, is sometimes used. The story is also told that Mzilikazi, the Zulu King and chief of a great army, who arrived in this area in 1840, named the dome-shaped hills after his many bald headed indunas (warriors). Perhaps in his imagination he saw their glistening pates, like granite domes, marching across the imposing landscape.

These hills, which lie 30km south-east of Bulawayo, are the furthermost western extremity of a granite shield extending from north to south on the eastern side of Zimbabwe. As already discussed, they are marginally isolated by surrounding flat lands, thus creating a geological island. The hills extend for 100km from the Mangwe Pass in the west to Mbalabala in the east, and are approximately 30km at their widest point.

Many Matopo hills have apt descriptive local names linked very often to myths and traditions. Bambata cave was first recorded, archaeologically, by Neville Jones and the hill owes its name to a Zulu verb 'ugubambata' meaning to caress or stroke. This is associated with the story that Mzilikazi once ascended this hill and, finding himself unable to retrace his steps descended on all fours, in so doing, stroking the granite with his hands.[2]

The Ififi mountain is named after the Mzilikazi Roller (also known as the Lilac-breasted Roller) as in certain lights there is a resemblance to the glorious blues of this bird.

Inungu, the porcupine, in hunched profile, stands guard at the northern end of Maleme dam.

Gali in the Golati communal lands means 'a beer pot' in the language of the Barozwi.

One of the first great granite mountains one sees to the left, on driving into the National Park, towering above the broad valley of the Mtsheleli river, is Imadzi, meaning 'near a swamp'; and Pomongwe – the melon – as named by the Kalanga, rises above the great cavity of its famous cave. Njelele, one of the highest points, is closely connected with the worship of Ngwali wa Matopo, "the God of the Matopo hills", a supreme being and creator of the universe. This god, Mwari in Shona, Mlimo in Ndebele, is not seen and his medium who resides at Njelele may only be approached by spiritual leaders interceding for and conveying messages from their people. This is a place of spiritual meaning for many throughout the country.

A story is told that this deity jumped across the Matopo to the sacred hill of Njelele and in so doing left his footprint between the hills of Kalanyoni and Nswatugi – "the place of jumping".

The shorter nose may indicate a Black Rhino. The Matopo is one of the last refuges of the heavily poached Black and White Rhinos.

Monkeys occur far less frequently than baboons. These appear as white images in a shelter with many other white paintings.

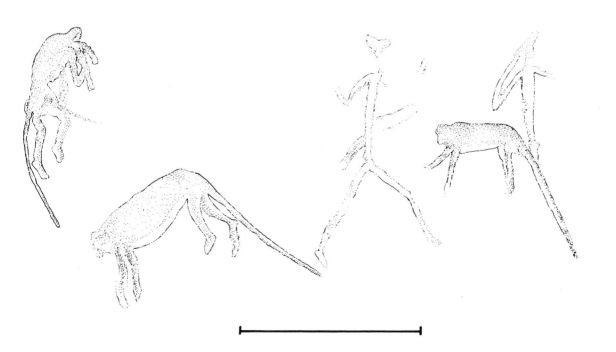

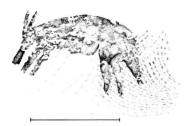

The hidden hunters, with lion heads, can only be seen by lying flat and peering under a rocky overhang. There are many small painted sites nearby and the valley terminates in a large painted cave.

The realistic antbear is shown in close association with the remains of broken lines which may represent ants.

Every hill is named and many are venerated, and custom dictates that specific hills should not be pointed at with the index finger. It is thought that non-adherence to this taboo precipitates cold and inclement weather.

The Ancient Landscape

This present Matopo landscape was formed three million years ago deep underground, but the origins of the granite forms remain speculative. Today we see the Matopo in a transitional period between the initial flat plain of many million years ago and the final leveling that will be brought about so many million years from now. In the far distant past, before humankind arrived on earth, we would have seen here a bleak and desolate plain, but today it is our good fortune to find a splendid landscape of hills and valleys carved out and created by the continuous action of erosion and weathering. All this we see today remained buried for many thousands of years, and was only slowly uncovered to reveal the present Matopo hills.

It is considered that the main erosion process is sub-surface chemical weathering in which water plays the major part and is the single most important factor at work. This underground process proceeds regardless of climatic conditions at the surface but, once exposed to air, moisture attack is reduced in the dry climate of the Matopo and the weathering process slows. The combined pervasive forces of water reacting with granitic chemicals eat into the weaknesses of the granite, transforming the rock into the present shapes and forms we see today. Joints or fractures are the means whereby water further infiltrates the granite and accelerates the weathering. Now we see massive granite domes, elliptical extrusions aptly termed 'whalebacks' (or Dwalas, the Sindebele word for a large rock) and great jumbled blocks of broken granite called 'castle kopjes' (kopje being the Afrikaans word for hill). These kopjes feed the imagination, conjuring up human and animal forms – Cecil Rhodes in his armchair; a woman carrying a baby on her back; prehistoric creatures; and a myriad of magical shapes.

In the mind these boulders seem to represent a mother and child and an elephant below.

A weathering feature that takes place above ground is known as exfoliation. In this process the rock which was formed in concentric layers and is then subjected to daily wide-ranging temperatures, (up to 30° centigrade variations in the Matopo) becomes susceptible to splitting along its joints, the rock falling away like peeling layers of onion skin to lie in jumbled piles below.[3] Very minimal destruction by weathering above ground has occurred, and it is of interest that during the author's 16 years of field work, no rock falls have been heard or witnessed – the change in landforms are not perceivable in one's lifetime. The environment is surprisingly stable. One is looking at an almost timeless landscape. Little has changed since the Matopo Bushmen, nurtured by the endless bounty, lived within the caves and shelters.

A typical "whaleback" – the granite dome over Pomongwe cave.

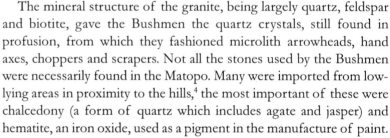

A typical "castle kopje".

Sable antelope

The mineral structure of the granite, being largely quartz, feldspar and biotite, gave the Bushmen the quartz crystals, still found in profusion, from which they fashioned microlith arrowheads, hand axes, choppers and scrapers. Not all the stones used by the Bushmen were necessarily found in the Matopo. Many were imported from low-lying areas in proximity to the hills,[4] the most important of these were chalcedony (a form of quartz which includes agate and jasper) and hematite, an iron oxide, used as a pigment in the manufacture of paint.

The hills intercept the prevailing south and south-easterly rain clouds making precipitation higher than in the surrounding areas and giving rise to a profuse and diverse plant life. Here we have a sanctuary of almost unlimited diversity in a relatively small area, an island oasis surrounded by grasslands. The granite slopes provided caves and shelters – the Bushmen's refuge; open but restricted grassland – home to the smaller antelope; boulder-strewn granite hillsides sheltering large populations of dassies, which were trapped and eaten by the Bushmen. An aquatic environment brought about by the configuration of granite boulders which act as reservoirs for the water slowly seeping away to create marshy areas and hidden pools. A year-round water supply for today's inhabitants and the pre-historic people before them.

The rich humic soils nurture many known indigenous edible plants,[5] a number of which would have been utilised by the Bushmen to maintain a varied diet; and so we can see the strength of the Matopo lies in its wealth of resources, relatively predictable seasons and availability of water.

The rocky shelters and densely wooded valleys provide the ideal habitat for reptiles, birds and the smaller species of mammal and, as Walker points out, "... the Matopos has the more diverse fauna but

lay grain bins built by subsequent Bantu farmers are frequently built against painted walls and up against painted ceilings.

amage by exfoliation during fire.

Indiscriminate digging by a tour operator to uncover stone age artefacts (see below).

typical castle kopje.

Originally extensively painted, this long sloping cave has the astonishing line of at least six hundred impala.

A pinnacle of granite, the perch for a pair of black eagles on the summit with small shelters at the base; originally painted but all the images are degraded.

A typical cave sheltering the paintings found on p.115

One of the few painted scenes that might be described as a battle.

This elegant female figure with flowing skirt appears below the battle scene depicted above.

The clarity of the snake, animals and humans on the rock is astonishing (see p. 40).

Possibly one of the highest painted sites in the Matopo and illustrated on pp. 60/61.

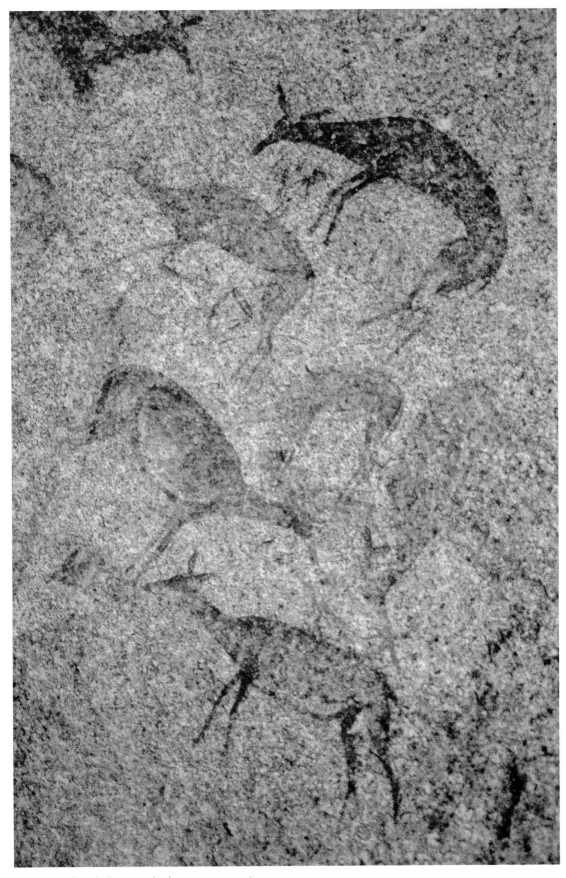

The group of gambolling impala that appear on p. 47.

An unusual depiction of children carried on the shoulders and shown on page 49.

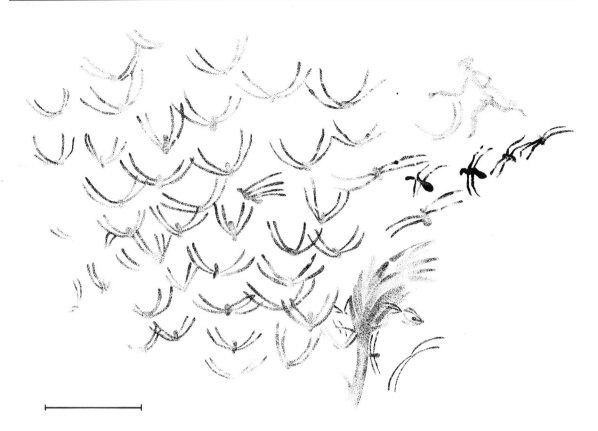

lacks the large herds of the other areas [Lowveld and Hwange].... The Matopos can therefore be regarded as relatively unsuitable for ungulates, owing to the amount of kopje and dense vegetation."[6]

Snakes abound and, not surprisingly, the Bushmen wove them into their mythology. The painted images live side by side with the reality of cobras, puff adders and mambas, the latter often achieving great diameter and length. 68 reptile and 28 amphibian species have been identified in the Matopo area,[7] the python taking pride of place for size and food capacity. This massive snake can attain a length of 5m and consume a female bushbuck! Achieving a length of 4m, the black mamba is common and very dangerous. If cornered it will rear up and strike. Be warned! If faced with this situation, stand still until the snake moves away. The venom is neurotoxic and deadly! The puff adder rarely exceeds 60cm in length but is responsible for 75% of serious snake bites in Africa as it relies on its excellent camouflage to escape detection, lying beside paths to ambush rodents and unwary humans!

Despite the reliable water supply and fertile slopes and valleys, only 6% of the total area is suitable for agriculture. In 1920, Dr E.A. Nobbs who was then Director of Agriculture wrote, "The land being intrinsically poor in the extreme, excessively rugged, largely mere rock

There are swarms of flying termites on two of the three fire-damaged shelter walls. Although not drawn with anatomical correctness, a feeling of swarming has been captured. Flying ants are eaten by indigenous people and the small figure holds an object as shown on p. 106, for smoking out bees.

There are faded remains of many paintings on a long wall nearby but in this small and secret cave the images are wonderfully clear. Snake, man and antelope integrated.

with small patches of infertile soil between. It is too favoured by baboons for cropping and too tiger [leopard] haunted for stock, too water logged in summer and too cold and exposed in winter. The land is therefore for purposes of production of little or no value."[8] Allowing for this fact it would seem reasonable that the Matopo would be suited for a National Park as a means of protecting the unique environment and, in 1953, 250 000 acres were designated for this purpose. The people were moved out, reluctantly and bitterly they went, leaving their spiritual and ancestral home. Unfortunately, the resentment thereby generated lingers to this day.

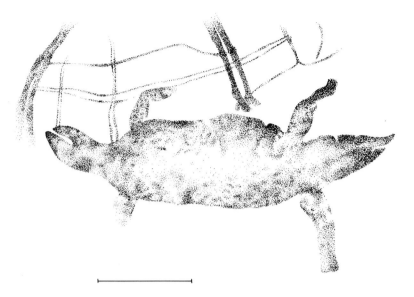

Crocodiles appear infrequently and this image is faded and fragmented. The shelter lies between two rivers and today a large crocodile alternates between the two and must pass quite close to the painting when changing abode.

Within the newly established National Park a small Game Park was created and many animals re-introduced. Prior to this, the hills had been all but denuded of game by uncontrolled hunting and poaching. The programme of game re-introduction was, in part, influenced by the animals which appear in the Bushmen's paintings and you will see today most of the animals they saw, in a scene that has changed little in two thousand years.

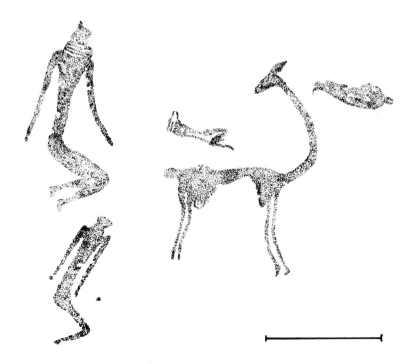

This was originally interpreted as a Gerenuk or Dibatag antelope although it is highly improbable that these north African species could have been seen by the Bushmen. This painting is degraded which may account for the appearance of the figure on all fours with the buck's head emanating from the buttocks. The disks on the neck of the seated figure are described in Garlake's Hunter's Vision, *Chapter 7, and attributed to a sensation experienced in trance, or are they body adornments?*

Over the years these complex images have been much reproduced but there is no satisfactory explanation or interpretation. One can only marvel at their clarity and diversity. The 'fish pond' and swimming figures appear to be realistic but a small flying 'alite' adds a touch of unreality.

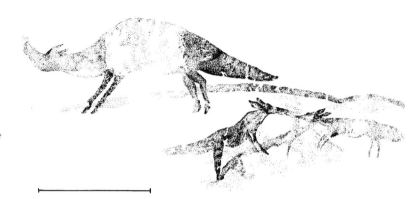

A depiction of an apparently real life scene and by coincidence, in the Bulawayo Museum, four jackals have been mounted on display in similar stance, the youngsters fighting over a bird and the adult standing guard.

Since prehistoric times the hills have been used as a shelter and refuge, providing a utopian existence for the hunter-gatherers and then as a hideaway for succeeding races. The fantastic rock formations amongst which grow an amazing variety of plants, fed by hidden water seeps and springs and providing the ideal habitat for a great diversity of insects, birds and mammals, make up a largely unknown ecosystem. This gloriously diverse landscape holds yet another treasure – the Bushmen's paintings. A perfect gallery for the elusive and puzzling drawings. In them we see the unchanged face of history – only the Bushmen gone – the missing link.

Maleme Valley

Like fishing terns, black eagles fold their wings
And dive headfirst off the kopje-tops
Into blue space, to drawl elliptic rings
Through early light. In a still copse
One branch thrashes wildly and dun-green
Figures ambling on their knuckles hoist lean
Rumps and vanish in the grass.
All these rocks knocked into shape by days!
A dwala peels, a tip-toe boulder cranes
Into space that sweeps down into the vleis
Where a seep of milky water drains
To green fur-lined pools where quartz veins flash.
Here once a year stormwaters waltz and thrash
And sink to feed the patient grass.
The kopje-tops bask in pinkish light.
Gold spills up from the black cut-out west.
The sky is aquarium-green, then night.
A shooting star zips over the hillcrest,
Trailing smoke. Leopard coughs, owl perceives,
Night snake slides into the leaves.
The prows of kopjes forge through seas of grass.

ROWLAND MOLONY

5

Life was for Living

"To live much of one's life in the same small community in the unprivate intimacy of a band and to have the life long habit of attending not only to what is said but also to a wide spectrum of indications of how it is said must sharpen perception to a degree that we, perhaps, cannot even imagine."

GEORGE SILBERBAUER

Let us go back in time to the emergence of our hunter-gatherers in Africa, the wanderers who for thousands of years and until comparatively recent times, lived a nomadic existence. In sub-Saharan Africa extremes of environment have always been experienced, making the transition to agriculture and herding a difficult adaptation; but these people roamed Africa in apparent harmony with nature possibly surviving more successfully than humans have done since and may do in the future.

Our present day Bushmen in the Kalahari, although fragmented and marginalised, must still bear a resemblance to their ancestors, the people of the Matopo; but contact with the European immigrants in South Africa has eroded the fragility of the San culture and, as Laurens van der Post understood intuitively, the Bushman "... was essentially so innocent and natural a person that he had only to come near us for a sort of radio-active fall-out from our unnatural world to produce a fatal leukemia in his spirit."[1] Unfortunately, the Matopo Bushmen disappeared so long ago that all memories of them are gone, no oral history exists, and there has been little documented archaeological exploration; but using the work of recent ethnologists in the Kalahari (Marshall, Silberbauer, Shapera), we can only assume that the lifestyle 2 000 years ago in the Matopo was in many ways comparable to that recorded by these researchers and found in similar isolated hunter-gatherer societies still in existence today.

With some trepidation one takes the Kalahari Bushmen as a role model, but we have no alternative as in this century these are the only hunter-gatherers in Southern Africa. Therefore it is a reasonable

No ordinary hunters, these men have antelope heads, horns and tails and an exaggerated lengthening of the body.

A typical spheroidal shelter.

assumption that in the Matopo a similar life-style existed but influenced by a very different environment. The Kalahari desert is vast, lightly vegetated and parched. The Matopo is contained, plant life is prolific and even in drought years water is available. In the desert the San move with the seasons and the availability of plants, animals and water but even under these conditions it was found by the anthropologist, George Silberbauer, that few people, "... have any knowledge of geography beyond a radius of 250 km and the personal experience of most is limited to a range of about 80 km."[2]

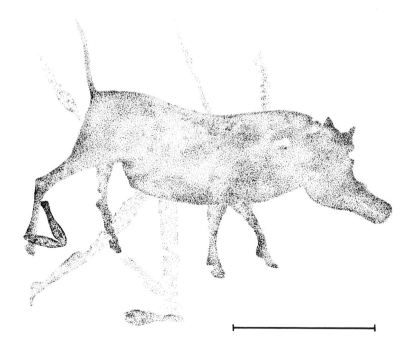

The erect tail and hurrying gait – the "jizz" of the warthog.

Seasonal migrations any distance from the Matopo would, on the basis of Kalahari research and our knowledge of the plentiful Matopo resource base, seem improbable. In the well watered Matopo, a storehouse of vegetable and protein foodstuffs, extensive movement out of the hills for provisions would have been unnecessary, and we can assume the existence of a more sedentary lifestyle.

Rocky enclaves within the hills have been a refuge and home for humans over thousands of years, and these caves and shelters, large and small, gave the Bushmen protection from the wind, rain and sun.

Anthropologists have shown the San of the Kalahari to be a society closely involved with and adapted to their natural environment. These people utilised their habitat but Silberbauer emphasises the critical fact that the San did not "... obtain their food by manipulating the productivity of their environment. They live off its unimproved resources and are entirely dependent upon uncultivated, untended plants and wandering wild animals for their food".[3] Unlike present day

Painted on the ceiling, these impala are immaculate, being protected from human, animal and climatic assault. A painting of a young antelope suckling is an infrequent occurrence although there is another in Amadzimba cave in the Matopo, and in the Brandberg, Namibia. (see Cambridge Illustrated History of Prehistoric Art, *Bahn, p. 190)*

communities who carry environmental exploitation to its final destruction and collapse, these hunter-gatherers took only a calculated part and left the residue to regenerate. Humans were seen as an integral non-dominant part of this structure, a jigsaw puzzle of great complexity, finely balanced to benefit all the participants – plants, animals and people.

The close social system based on a network of relationships was extended to include the many organisms found in the Bushmen's physical environment, bringing humans into an intimate psychological relatedness with all living matter. Survival was very much dependent upon an acute sense of observation – all knowledge was, of necessity, memorised and in this non-literate society intensive verbal communication was essential. Silberbauer gives us an intimate picture of San life and after many years of close observation saw that the group size influenced its viability for, "The collective memory of the 20–30 adults in a band is much more than ten times as rich in retrievable knowledge as would be the case if there were only two or three adults in a group of six or seven individuals."[4] Each band member contributed to the communal memory notebook upon which the whole framework of daily living depended. This necessity could explain the lack of hierarchical placings and tribal structures within clans, for it was recognised that every member was of equal importance.[5] This dispersed leadership does not obviate the need for unobtrusively recognised leaders, differing clan members acting as advisors during times of decision making, stress or conflict.

Social interaction between neighbouring bands extended the means for further obtaining and disseminating information and the whole social structure was founded on a highly defined interactive interdependence. This characteristic feature of 'give and take' led to harmonious relations and co-operation within the band. These conditions of social stability and lack of conflict were essential to survival. Researchers in the Kalahari found that these attitudes led to an extensive aversion to physical violence; however, as Richard Leakey points out, "The absence of indications of intergroup violence before the agricultural revolution does not of course prove that our hunter-gatherer ancestors earlier than 10 000 years ago were not as violent and as inclined to genocide as they have been in recent times. As always in science, the absence of evidence cannot be taken to be evidence of absence. But I take it to be a very reasonable inference."[6] And we can too, for there are few scenes of violent human behaviour, murder or assault in the Matopo paintings.

It would seem from observation and research of existing hunter-gatherer societies that they are egalitarian by nature, with an accepted delineation of roles, living in harmony and co-operation. According to Silberbauer, the Kalahari Bushmen's "... view of the nature of man is consistent with their desire for harmony in their social relationships. The noun stem khwe – can be translated as "man" in the general sense. Its use implies possession of the qualities of g//ahasi (friendliness), mahasi (generosity), anxasi (wisdom), and (!wamsi) calmness and good humour. To lack these qualities is to be dubbed khwemkjima'a (man-not-is, i.e., inhuman). Known ethnic categories consist of people who are regarded as being inherently good, and there is the expectation of finding these qualities in them."[7]

These animated figures appear in one of a series of small caves. This is a highly unusual scene in which it would seem a child is being carried on the backs of both the male and female figures. A photograph of a !Kung San woman and child, taken in the 70s by Richard Lee, replicates these images.

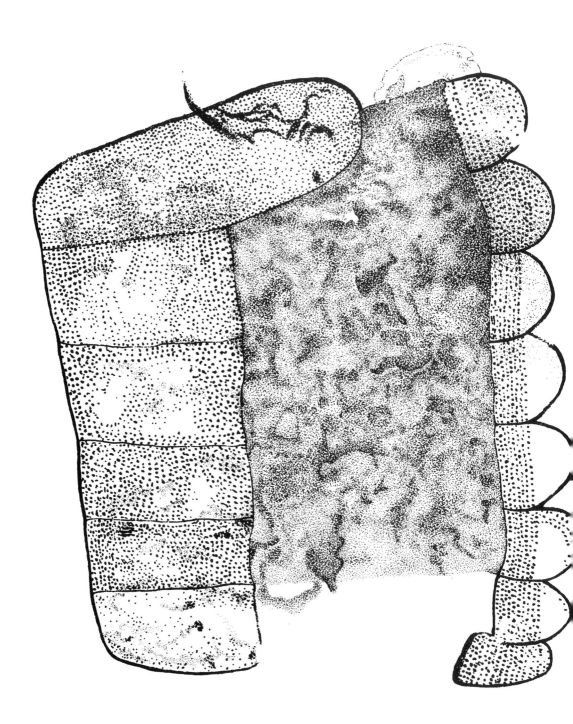

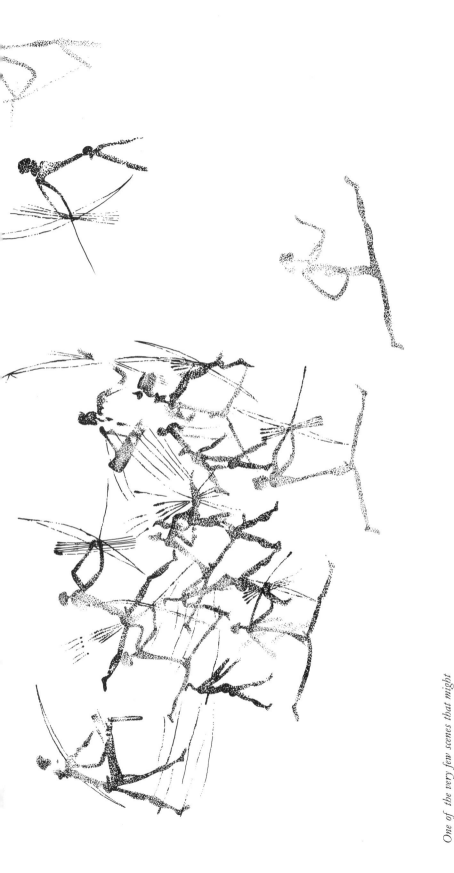

One of the very few scenes that might be interpreted as a battle. There are only two similar compositions known to the author in the Matopo. Here we see two definite types of human figures, some with long slim bodies and human heads, while the others are shorter, stockier and hook-headed. All are closely associated with the dominant elliptical form.

This woman and small male figure, possibly a child, are the very clear remains on a series of walls originally heavily painted. This is an unusually anatomically correct representation of the classic Bush-woman with increased lumbar curve, marked steatopygia and holding a digging stick.

On the rock the significance of the expanded arrowheads is emphasised by the contrasting colours. The heads are pale pink and burnt sienna. The painting loses much by not being reproduced in colour.

Time and again, researchers have emphasised the non-violent nature of the hunter-gatherer society. Elizabeth Marshall Thomas, travelling in the Kalahari in the early 1950s, realised that, "Bushmen cannot afford to fight with each other and almost never do because their only real weapon is their arrow poison, for which there is no antidote. But even were they to disregard this danger, Bushmen would try not to fight because they have no mechanism in their culture for dealing with disagreements other than to remove the causes of the disagreements."[8]

The Gatherer-Hunters

It is known that hunter-gatherers operate in small nomadic bands, and it has been postulated that, in the Matopo, clans would have been unlikely to exceed 25 people.[9] While these bands maintained social and economic interaction with neighbouring groups there was little reason to wander very much further afield, possibly moving only short distances to take advantage of seasonal variations in flora and fauna. On occasion they may have ventured into the surrounding flat land to hunt plains game, but under normal, stable social conditions, the hills would have provided food in ample sufficiency.

Today's Kalahari San consume 60–80% of vegetable matter in their daily diet, contrary to a popular misconception that these people are primarily hunters and mainly meat eaters. A misnomer – these are gatherer-hunters!! The proportion of time spent daily collecting food in the Kalahari is relatively small, estimated to be less than three hours per day, per adult[10] and it is a mistaken belief that collecting food imposed demanding constraints upon their time and that it was necessary to collect and hunt throughout the daylight hours. More especially in the Matopo, the bounty of foodstuffs would have allowed for a relatively leisurely lifestyle and many researchers of the few remaining hunter-gatherer communities, still untainted by present day societies, speak of their relaxed lifestyle, good humour and generosity. Not for Bushmen the stress and pace of modern day living!

It has been shown in the Kalahari that although meat constitutes a smaller proportion of the hunter-gatherers' food, hunting is of great cultural significance. Hunting can still be a means of acquiring higher rank but there is evidence in the paintings that the bow and arrow was not only a tool or a weapon of aggression, but also a symbol. The expanded arrowhead, quite impractical for killing, was possibly painted as a visual icon of information.

Within the valleys grazing is limited but sufficient to attract the smaller antelope, and the rocky kopjes are a refuge for dassies, rabbits,

An excellent example of expanded arrowheads. An isolated image in a series of painted sites on a long low kopje.

reptiles, tortoises and small cats. All would have played their part in stocking the Bushmen larder but, as the great poetic writer, Laurens van der Post, born in 1906 and brought up in Bushmenland, South Africa, observed, "Before we all came to shatter his natural state I have never found true evidence that he exceeded his proportions. His killing, like the lion's, was innocent because he killed only to live. He never killed for fun or the sake of killing, and even when doing it was curiously apprehensive and regretful of the deed. The proof of all this is there in his paintings on his beloved rock for those who can see with their hearts as well as their eyes."[11]

It is known that the climate in southern Africa would have changed from 29 000 to 15 000 BP with cooler conditions during the glacial periods. The archaeologist Nick Walker, states that, "It is thus postulated that the present Park vegetation is unlikely to be appreciably different from that in pre-Iron Age times" although proportions and dominance in the overall vegetation composition would have altered; but that, "... even quite appreciable climatic changes are unlikely to have altered the overall plant community."[12] We can assume that the climate in the halcyon days of the Late Stone Age Bushmen in the Matopo varied little from present day conditions, the hills as rich then as they are to-day in edible fruits, leaves, tubers and berries, with at least sixty differing species recorded and undoubtedly others to be discovered.[13] Many fruits, especially the marula, are found in abundance; highly nutritious and easily gathered, they must have been used as a staple in a largely

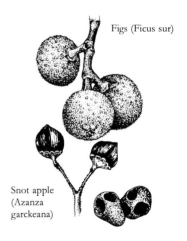

Figs (Ficus sur)

Snot apple (Azanza garckeana)

Maurla pips (Sclerocarya birrea)

Examples of edible fruit found in the Matopo.

A family of Dassies warming in the early morning sun.

The reality of known animals in association with a mythical antelope.

Interpretation of this image ranges from a hallucinatory experience to representation of a mythological being (see page 84).

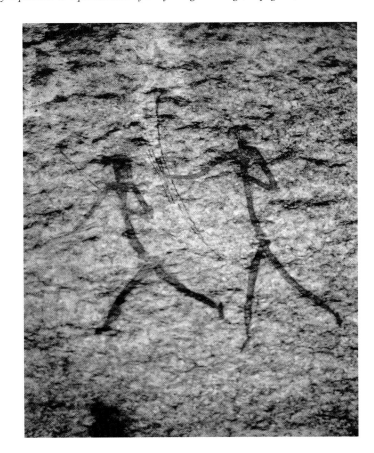

The solitary hunters walk or hurry across the rock.

The zoomorphic being that appears on page 79.

A recumbent eland painted very low down in an apse-like recess (page 78).

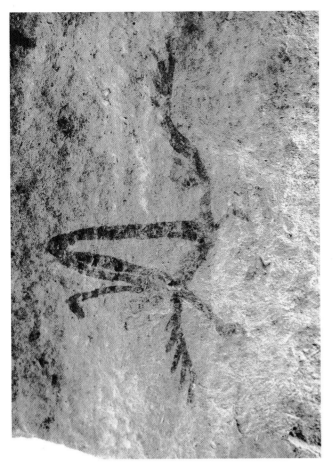

The therianthropic vulture that appears on page 91.

An unusually stocky figure runs along a wavy line that could be the back of one of the large Matopo serpents.

The many female figures in this high and secluded cave are depicted in stunning clarity and appear on pages 100/101.

Two one-legged figures (page 109) now seen by the local people as a bad omen.

The destructive effect of lichen is here well demonstrated by the small dots of yellow growth starting to obliterate the paint (see page 119

...ody paint is well illustrated on this leaping figure in Nswatugi cave (see page 12).

...part of the immense spread of painting in Nanke cave, and illustrated on page 25.

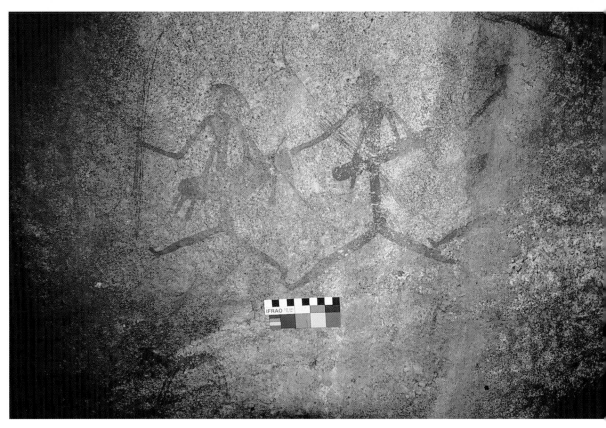

Two running hunters, the clear remains of a line of hunters as illustrated on page 20.

The enigmatic sickle-headed figures that defy interpretation.

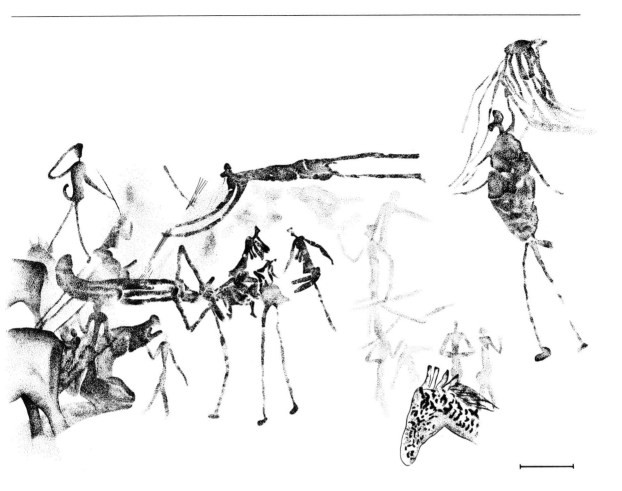

vegetarian diet, for Walker also found on excavation in the Matopo that, "Enormous piles of shelled marula stones have been recovered from some sites, and it seems likely that in some periods marula nuts were collected to be used during the rest of the year."[14]

Many animals seen in the Matopo today have been found in excavations, which provides further evidence that the climate and therefore the habitat have remained the same. Archaeologically it has been found that the dassie has consistently been consumed in large numbers in the Matopo. This prolific small mammal, resembling a squat brown, short-eared rabbit, perfectly adapted to the rocky habitat, has been preyed upon over the centuries by leopard, raptor and humans, yet with no obvious depletion to its numbers. To this day the dassie is the main prey of the resident leopards and black eagle, and the local communal farmers utilise the pelt and meat. These small animals live singly or gregariously, their behaviour, easily anticipated, making trapping and hunting a relatively easy task for the alert Bushmen.

The jumble of bodies and long thin disembodied legs are in striking contrast to the reality of the giraffe who seems a very ordinary chap. (The complete giraffe image appears on p. 108.) The bloated anthropomorphic figure on the right, with tail and muzzled face, is unusual in the Matopo, but found in the north of the country. (See Garlake, The Hunter's Vision, p. 89.) The two outstretched figures may be levitating or lying down. These are the clearest remains of a heavily painted large cave which could have been used either as a living or ceremonial shelter.

Now turn to the paintings and a striking fact emerges – there are no images of dassies or marulas. We are not looking at a comprehensive menu, the daily diet of the Bushmen. Although some of the animals hunted are depicted and there is an abundance of trees which may signify dietary habits or hallucinogenic plants, the many enigmatic and indecipherable images have led researchers to postulate that the paintings hold a deeper and more significant meaning.

Groovy Bones and Bushmen Bodkins

These people of the Late Stone Age made small stone tools and also utilised tortoise shells, ostrich eggs, bone and wood. Carefully crafted beads, eyed bone matting needles and bone tools, tubes and spatulas have been found in abundance during excavations. It has been suggested that small animal skins, arrow heads and reed mats could have been used in trade for hematite and ready-made ostrich eggshell beads as, on excavation, broken shell has not been found in association with beads which points to this ornamental item being imported. Very unusually, cordage, a material that degrades rapidly and is seldom found, was also excavated which lends weight to the theory of animal capture by trapping and snaring.

Carefully crafted microlith arrow heads were bound to wooden shafts and smeared with poison. The San in the Kalahari utilise the poisonous pulp of the larvae from three species of 'flea beetle' (Halticinae) but it is the larva of the ground beetle, *Lebistina*, which parasitises these flea beetles, that is considered to have the strongest and most effective poison. The Matopo have not been extensively researched and these beetles have not been recorded in the area but there is a strong possibility that they could occur, as Marula and several species of Paperbark trees – the foodplant of these beetles – are found in abundance.

Paperbark tree
(Commiphora marlothii)

Ostrich egg jewellery, bone sewing implements, cordage, and bone spatula.

The early missionary and explorer, Robert Moffat, during his travels through South Africa, observed in 1842 that, "The poisonous as well as noxious serpents, they roast and eat. They cut off the head of the former which they dissect and carefully extract the bags, or reservoirs of poison, which communicate with the fangs of the upper jaw. They mingle it with the milky juice of the Euphorbia or with that of a poisonous bulb. After simmering for sometime on a slow fire, it acquires the consistency of wax, with which to cover the points of the arrow."[15]

The poisons work slowly but are deadly. An arrow head many hundreds of years old and placed in a Museum as an exhibit is known to have induced rapid death in a rat! (Curators beware!) Although meat was of secondary importance, poison was essential for a kill but could take days to be effective. Endless tracking at high energy cost to the hunter was a labour-intensive exercise, and the meat that was not

Poison from the pupae of the Lebistina *beetle being smeared onto the shaft of an arrow.*

An unusual image in a richly painted area of low kopje sites. The long line emanating from the hunter's head could suggest trance associated with hunting potency – the arrows being infected with power. Alternatively, this is exactly as the San of the Kalahari dress their arrows with the poison from the pupae of the Lebistina *beetle, laying the arrows across a log of wood to dry over the fire, all the while relating past hunts and hopes for success in the future. (See* The Bushmen, *by Wannenburgh, Johnson and Bannister, p. 61)*

consumed on the spot had to be carried home, a further burden – small wonder that plant food constituted the bulk of the daily diet, and how much easier it is to send the women out to work!

Bridging the Real and the Unreal

In the Kalahari the dance is the central focus of clan life and essential to the band's cohesion, a lifeline establishing and maintaining coping mechanisms for the daily problems encountered, and the joy of escape in dance releases tensions and conflict within the community. The trance dance provides the ritualistic symbolism of a religious need and one could read into the Matopo paintings that the hunter-gatherers of long ago used similar procedures to enhance and retain group stability.

In the Matopo, did the shaman/healers, as in the Kalahari, bridge the real and unreal worlds of the community, reinforcing the bonds between the people, healing, reducing stressful tensions and influencing hunting, thus providing a focal point of stability and unification? This will be further explored in Chapter 7, but any attempts to link the paintings with existing or recorded mythology in Southern Africa must be placed without doubt in the realms of pure speculation. Recently, J.S. Kruger wrote that, "Even within the very small time frame of the 20th century Bushman beliefs vary considerably from epoch to epoch, from group to group, and even from individual to individual .... The anthropological accounts cover only the 19th and 20th centuries, but the general picture may apply to the earlier periods as well".[16] These accounts encompass our knowledge of the G\wi, our role models, and we know from this documentation that their

These tiny images seem to express the inter-relatedness of mammal, bird, reptile and man in the Bushmen's world. The dogs lose their forelegs and become birds; the human heads acquire bird and animal characteristics; the clubbed feet could mimic the birds' heads. A hidden shelter in which no other paintings remain.

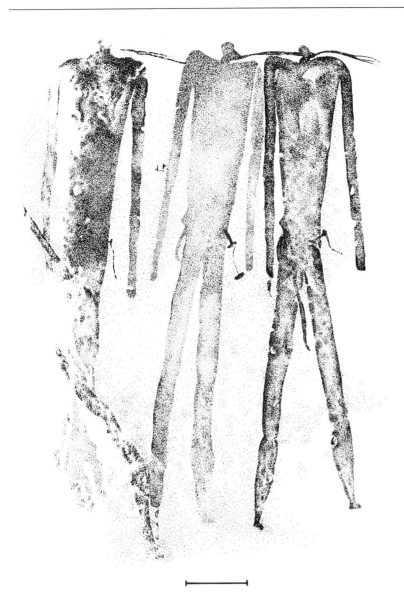

The importance of male gender has been emphasised by placing the penis on the side while the figures are forward facing. Pin heads and emanations from the mouth could be interpreted as signs of trance. Each figure is painted alternatively in ochre and burnt sienna.

religious ethic was limited to a reverence for N'Adima, a fickle god who rules in unpredictable ways, creating the universe and all life forms.[17]

All beings are bound within this rule, the mammals being most closely allied to man. The emphasis is placed upon the important relationship between man and animal, and in the rock paintings the blending of images, whether by over-painting or the deliberate creation of a therianthropic creature, points to a close cultural link. Here possibly we have a religious belief, though the paintings reveal no hint of a deity but perhaps a reverence and acknowledgment of parity. In

the classic study of magic and religion, *The Golden Bough*, Sir James George Frazer perceived that, "... to the savage, who regards all living creatures as practically on a footing of equality with man, the act of killing and eating an animal must wear a very different aspect from that which the same act presents to us, who regard the intelligence of animals as far inferior to our own and deny them the possession of immortal souls."[18]

Simple yet complex, to us an alien way of life but by understanding this forgotten culture can we 'look and learn'? Here are lessons for us in living with and not only taking from the environment; an interaction to achieve sustainability; a greater tolerance and a lessening of conflict for the common good. There is no going back to the way they lived, but many of these characteristics are enviable and thought-provoking. To appreciate and understand all this the paintings must not be viewed in isolation. Look at the whole picture. These images would seem to be an integral part of a complex and intricate way of life.

The site of these paintings is unusually high, above a deep river valley. They could represent a clan-gathering around a central fire, the figures sitting, reclining and dancing. BUT 'new age' interpretation would favour a shamanistic ritual.

6

A Testimony to Timeless, Technical Brilliance

"Art is a process of extending ourselves through our sensibilities and our imagination to something we have not reached before."

JULIAN HUXLEY

No man-made setting can compare with the great granite mountains, jumbled multi-coloured rocks, variegated plants and apparent infinity of the Matopo landscape, placing the paintings in the natural surroundings of a perfect gallery. Positioned on the rocks with care and expertise, the hunter-gatherers' delicate paintings show a sensitivity of style and application, attention to detail and the importance of image association. Here we see a seriousness of purpose, a tradition of drawing rather than painting, and therein lies its genius.

The boldly painted hunter is in sharp contrast to the ethereal dancers, their finely drawn bodies conveying rhythmical movement. There are many more outline figures, now indistinct.

These outline figures appear infrequently in the paintings. An area of exfoliation is shown on the lower two figures.

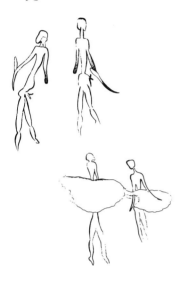

Rock art once belonged to the category known as "primitive art". Fortunately, this term is no longer used but, sadly, the stigma attached to the word 'primitive' still lurks in the shadows of people's understanding, conjuring up immediate and inaccurate prejudice. The word projected an altogether negative meaning, so often associated with things 'uncivilised' or second rate and, as is so often the case, because something is foreign to one's way of thinking or appears to be simple or non-intellectual, it is immediately dismissed as having no merit or purpose. Fortunately, a more enlightened approach now prevails.

With artwork it is a grave mistake to assume that simple art means a simple mind and we must beware of regarding the Bushmen as our intellectual inferiors, thereby assuming that our present day values are superior. These people had a heightened awareness of their surroundings and greater empathy with the natural world, sensual capacities which, to our cost, we have abandoned in our modern high-powered technological existence. The reader should now try to discard all preconceptions and look into the paintings with a receptive mind, open and uncluttered by previous prejudices and unsubstantiated ideas.

Of Painters, Palettes and Picasso

Line drawing is one of the most challenging art forms, as the single line has to convey form and mass and at the same time capture the essence and character of the object drawn; and so it is almost a paradox that this 'minimalistic' style can produce paintings of such density and

Part of a cluster of many small sites. Possibly the anatomical features were exaggerated to emphasise gender and animation.

vitality. The Matopo artwork meets all the requirements of well executed 'linear' art as can be seen in the Nswatugi Cave giraffe, (see above) where the painted images suggest the substance of a large animal without losing the fluidity of the giraffe's gait. The line drawings of human figures, though possibly intentionally less realistic, are no less full of life, and the many groups of people or animals moving in single file interact and flow naturally. These lines of figures, often painted on a descending slope, add to the feeling of movement and rhythm.

There is a definite feel for composition within the paintings particularly when more than two groups appear on one panel; and

This masterpiece in Nswatugi cave captures perfectly the long lolloping stride of the giraffe and, by contrast, the zebras upright brisk gait. The importance of the giraffe in the Matopo is emphasised by its appearance in all the major and many of the minor sites.

Trance or reality? Is the figure to the left lying in trance or just 'taking his ease'? The "trumpeter" plays his instrument or has an extended nose? (see p. 118). Long fingers, tails and lines from orifices, are these sensations of trancing? "Combs" may be unknown emblems, millipedes, or the Mopane worm, a delicacy harvested and eaten with relish to this day.

within these groups there is a curious interaction in that each group is a separate unit and yet part of the whole. In the big panels there is a sense of endlessness and freedom as there are no definite boundaries, visual or physical, to confine the groupings. This may be accentuated by another important characteristic of the art – no single viewpoint perspective, a device which, for the past 500 years has trained the eye to be drawn into a painting to a single vanishing point, thus giving the illusion of depth. By this omission the eye is free to move across the many varied images and is not held by one point of focus.

Confusion arises when the viewer is presented with a jumble of images painted partly or wholly on top of one another – termed 'superpositioning' (see page 92). These closely interwoven paintings may cover a shelter wall which is in close proximity to a smooth, clear, unpainted rock face, so it would appear that the relationship of the images one upon another was very particular and important and held symbolic meaning. Successive painters reinforced the imagery and, one could say, expanded the ritual of the story.

The question as to the significance of the rock face itself and the orientation of the surface to be painted is of interest. Can we say that the actual rock face chosen was significant? Research in many other parts of the world shows that the artists had often used the rock surface to emphasise form in the painted image, and there are instances where cracks or marks in the rock have been incorporated into the human or animal figure. Many art historians are certain that this cannot be ignored, and the South African artist and art historian, Pippa Skotnes, is of the opinion that, "The significance of the rock face

An example of how the obvious crack in the rock was not incorporated into the drawing.

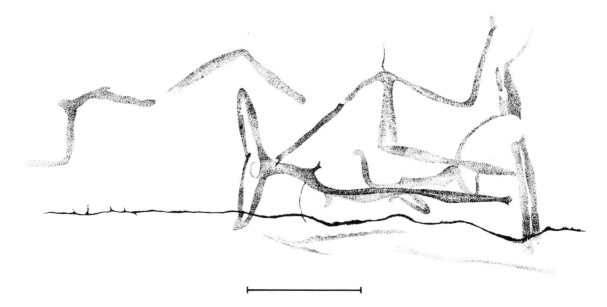

A symbol that appears in some of the more heavily painted larger caves and, one must assume, was recognised and understood. These crowded images show the close association of the real and the unreal in the Bushmen's world.

itself as a component part of the meaning of San painting, should come as no surprise."[1] This may be so elsewhere, but would seem not to apply to the Matopo paintings. Images appear on rough and smooth surfaces, in protected caves and on exposed rocks, and images have been painted over cracks and indentations with no attempt to incorporate them into the drawing. If the orientation of the site and the painted surface was meaningful in the Matopo, the reasons are obscure and unproven.

We can see so much in the Matopo paintings which would seem to be a direct reflection of the people and the 'minds' that created these images. Writing in *Origins Reconsidered*, the palaeoanthropologist Richard Leakey recognised the importance of the mind when he said, "We therefore must recognise [that] the archaeological record is, at best, only a guide to the past and especially that part of the past in which we are most interested, the workings of the mind."[2] It is an insight into the workings of an artist's mind that will help to explain and understand his paintings and himself. It also serves as a statement about the society to which the artist belongs, a fact that the eminent art historian E.H. Gombrich appreciated so many years ago for he saw that, "We cannot hope to understand these strange beginnings of art unless we try to enter into the mind of the primitive peoples and find out what kind of experience it is which makes them think of pictures, not as something nice to look at, but as something powerful to use."[3]

One is immediately aware of the unique characteristics and nuances achieved in the paintings. There is no real feeling of aggression in the art and even the most dynamic 'hunting scenes' show a sensitivity and almost naive gentleness, which surely must point towards an impression of these artists as being receptive, gentle people. No real horror, nothing that is negative or disturbing; but this does not mean that the paintings are without emotion. The complex scenes so often project a sense of awe and wonder and there is frequently a tangible awareness of the power surrounding these images, but it is very much a positive power, nothing sinister.

Many images appear to be related to mystical or unknown phenomena, and the author agrees with Pippa Skotnes that there is a complex inter-relationship in the Bushmen's life between the tangible and spirit worlds, for "The artwork does not describe the world, it is

A long low shelter in which also appear the outline figures on p. 63. It is difficult not to see a degree of unreality with the bucks' heads emanating from buttocks, a tail, head appendages and lines from armpits and head. The oval shape could be the remains of a larger form.

that world"[4] and the integration of these two worlds must be acknowledged if we are to try and understand the significance of the images.

The Bushmen artists remain anonymous unlike their counterparts today who seldom hesitate to sign their work; but the converse is true of the recent cubist painters who rejected this individualist approach and emphasised that the content of the composition was of greater importance. Writing in 1950, Herbert Read appreciated that primitive man regards art, "... as of such practical importance that its use is socialised; an artist for art's sake would probably be killed as a dangerous devil, but an artist for the community's sake becomes priest and king, for he is the maker of magic, the voice of the spirits, the inspired oracle, the intermediary through whom the tribe secures fertility for their crops or success for their hunters."[5] A pluralistic art within an egalitarian society unlike our individualistic egotistical culture of today.

Looking at the content of the paintings in the Matopo, there is no emphasis on individuality: the human form is representative, unemotional, defined by gender and equipment.

It has long been recognised that rock art is a form of 'conceptual art'. Cubism was born out of our modern idea of conceptual art, a reality beyond the scope of visual perception when, at the end of the 19th century, Paul Cezanne reverted to the conventions of dealing with space and perspective as 'the Primitives' had done thousands of years before. Picasso and Braque developed Cezanne's principles further as they attempted, "... to displace reality; reality was no longer in the object. Reality was in the painting."[6] and based their early cubist work on three main concepts: firstly, the painting of objects from different viewpoints at once; secondly, the volume and space around the object is just as important as the object itself; and thirdly, the idea of bringing everything into closer two-dimensional perspective and doing away with a single focal point.

All these ideas can be traced back to and seen in the Matopo rock art. Whatever one wants to call it, the Bushmen were totally unaware of, and quite unconcerned with, any specific categorisation of their work. They were not trying to be conceptual artists or cubists, they were just painting in a style that came naturally to them.

It would be unfair to assume that every viewer of rock art has an understanding or knowledge of art itself, but most people have an underestimated ability to react to a work of art with an intrinsic sense of its artistic worth. People say, "I don't know anything about art but I know what I like."! This is because all art is a form of communication and, whether or not one is aware of this, every work of art conveys a message to the viewer. If it speaks in a language one understands,

These two women wearing skirts, possibly carrying whisks and wearing a head dress, bear a strong resemblance to the female figure on p. 95. This is a good example of twisted perspective and the importance of emphasising gender.

These tailed hunters, their bodies full of lively expression, carry curious weighted arrows.

then we like it. If it appears unintelligible, as in a foreign tongue, we dismiss it. There is no point in reading *The Three Musketeers* in French if one only speaks and understands English, and although you may be told it is a great classic story, without a translation there is no meaningful understanding.

If no attempt is made to understand the paintings and the 'language' in which they are written, they too will be unintelligible. In effect, these paintings were written in a foreign tongue, a code to be deciphered and in this way, translated into an intelligible vocabulary.

Herbert Read had an intuitive understanding of 'the primitives', appreciating that the hunter-gatherers had "alternative methods of conceiving the world" and that "the artist expresses what he perceives; he perceives what he expresses."[7] In the approach to interpretation there are some assumptions and possibly some errors which must be open to a process of critical appreciation. The early researchers were still conditioned to seeing things subjectively: did they miss the symbolism in the rock art, seeing it only as decorative and representational? In this book we can only offer the many interpretations as a way to a better understanding of the Bushmen, their life and their art in the Matopo hills.

The Power of Paint

One can only marvel at the unconscious technical brilliance of the Bushmen artists. Many of the paintings executed more than 2000 years ago are still so visible that sometimes the clarity is breathtaking; but it has been known for centuries that earth pigments, a basic constituent of the paint, have great permanence. Earth pigments, also termed mineral or inorganic pigments, are made by refining naturally coloured clays and rocks and mixing them with a binding agent. Apart from the certainty that these pigments are notoriously long lasting, it is also a well established fact that combining them with egg makes a highly durable paint medium. Known as 'egg tempera' it is said to have been used by the Egyptians and Romans before becoming a refined and accepted technique for artists during the 14th and 15th centuries. Used by medieval craftsmen, egg tempera was simply made by grinding pigment and a little water to a thick paste, then adding sufficient egg yolk to do just the amount of painting necessary. The Bushmen would have most likely used the whole egg and, as albumen hardens when exposed to sunlight, this would have contributed to the known longevity of the paintings.

This is a soft medium, easy to apply and quick drying, but does not have good blending qualities, so that differing colours in close association will not merge. Admirably suited to a linear style of painting, and what could be more linear than the Matopo art?

Once dry, the paint layer becomes water resistant and no protective varnishes or coatings are needed. Exposed to air and sunlight it forms a tough adherent layer which has proved over the centuries to be the most durable of all paint films. Much external art exposed to the elements over thousands of years lives on as a clear testimony to the permanence of the paint.

Traditional watercolours are made from natural ingredients, all of which would have been available to the Bushmen, if in slightly differing forms. The 'binder' is gum arabic from the *Acacia arabica* tree, not found in the Matopo, but other gum bearing trees, including Acacias, occur in profusion. In particular, the Sweet thorn, (*Acacia karoo*) exudes an edible, clear, golden or red gum, providing a suitable and readily available binder.

Acacia karoo

This is too small a shelter for habitation but was extensively painted high above arm's reach, and looks out over a large grassy plain. These paintings are black and the elegance of movement in the archer is quite striking. Unusually, two of the male figures wear skirts. The shoulder bar and open neck are difficult to explain.

The 'plasticizer' which effects the compatibility of pigment to binder and overcomes brittleness is 'hydromel' – simply honey water.

The 'wetting' agent needed to facilitate an even flow of paint is oxgall – the bile from the gall bladders of cattle. Having no cattle, the Bushmen would have found the bile from kudu or eland just as effective.

The 'extender', a self-explanatory word, is any substance such as an inert pigment (e.g. chalk or gypsum) that, when added to paint, increases the bulk.

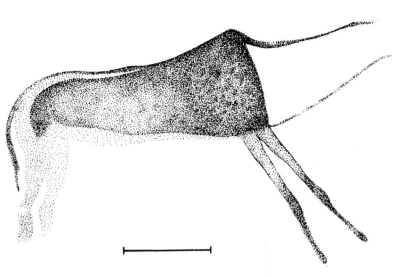

The contrasting colours of sienna and ochre give the impression of an inner and outer body. The fugitive white paint on the neck and possibly the head of the antelope has faded.

It is not suggested that the Bushmen had necessarily worked all this out and used all these ingredients together each time, but they were available and have been known and used for many years in the manufacture of good quality paints.

Hematite, the iron oxide mineral found naturally in the outskirts of the hills, was ground to a fine dust and produced the glorious browns and yellows of the artists' palette. This versatile pigment turns a rusty red when heated and gave the artist his most favoured colour.

Many of the black images are remarkable for their clarity and point to the use of charcoal, a pigment known for its enduring qualities. The assumption has been made that silica, china clay and gypsum were used to produce a white paint but this does not seem feasible as they are inert pigments, they have no colour qualities and in modern day paints are used only as extenders. There is, however, the possibility that china clay in the form of kaolin could have given a strong enough white hue but, being a clay, would not have adhered well to the rock surface. This is apparent in the fugitive nature of the white paint which makes careful observation of the images important. The painting may appear incomplete, part of the animal or human figure missing, but look carefully and you may see the faded remains of a white outline or infill, possibly changing the very nature of the painting.

By great good fortune the granite surface offers a particularly receptive and sympathetic medium to the paint which appears to be partly absorbed, possibly mixing with the granitic chemicals, these acting as a fixing agent thus reinforcing the longevity of the paintings.

There is some speculation as to the use of blood as a mixing agent and that by the incorporation of either human or animal blood both painting and painter would acquire power and potency. Researchers

No trace remains of what might have been white lower legs and the face appears to have been drawn 'trumpet' shaped, mimicking the human figures with extended 'nose' (pp. 117 and 118).

A line of 30 antelope cross below the albino leopard and cub; and a shelter within 10km has a similar line of the same impala – a staggering 600! Impala appear at many sites in the Matopo and this refutes Garlake's statement that they are rare. Animal spoor (to the left) are seldom seen and the expanded arrowheads are of unusual design.

have recently extracted animal DNA from fragments of 4 000 year old Texan rock paintings which lends credence to the ritualistic use of blood to reinforce animalistic/religious beliefs[8], but in the Matopo no paint analysis has been done. Possibly we can assume that the painter executed his art within the confines of a similar socio-religious system.

An early traveller in South Africa, during the last century, E.J. Dunn, saw Bushmen carrying prepared pigments in the horns of small antelope and, in the Matopo, stone palettes have been found in excavations but brushes, made of wood, hair and feathers, would not have survived the ravages of time. Porcupine quills may have been used to paint outlines.

Over the last 2 000 years cave floor levels have changed little so we must look elsewhere to explain the height of many paintings. The Bushmen must surely have used wooden ladders to execute their paintings as well as to reach honey combs, of great importance, situated in rocky crevices. A ladder made of wood and bark thongs by the local people, stood for years against the granite in the 'Cave of Bees' to give access to a hive in a high crevice.

The artists with their great technical ability were placed in a pivotal

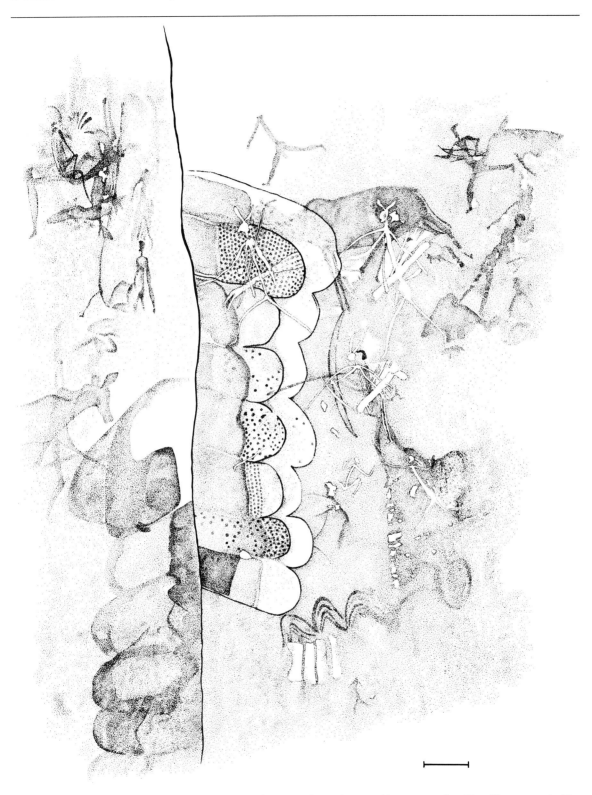

This cave and associated shelters are densely painted and a group of impala on p. 47 appear on the ceiling. These unusual white hunters are closely associated with the elliptical imagery. The crack serves as a base line for these images which are drawn on both sides although faded on the left.

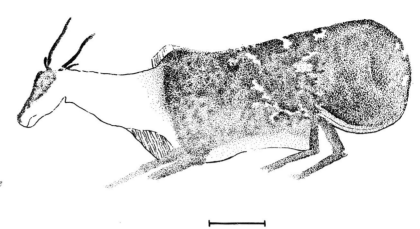

An exact representation of a recumbent eland although, unfortunately, the striking contrast of ochre and white colouring is lost in this reproduction.

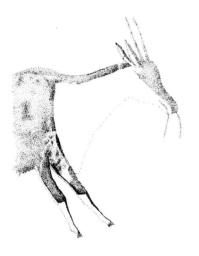

position within the society and, as Julian Huxley reminds us, "The individual artist has two main functions – that of creator and that of interpreter. As interpreter, he translates complex and emotion-tinged experience into directly communicable forms and so is able to express what otherwise would remain inexpressible."[9]

The accumulated historical wisdom of their culture is recorded on the rocks. Without these drawings there would have been no revelations or interpretations of the cultural intricacies of the Bushmen's life.

Unlike South Africa where the eland is the dominant antelope drawn, here in the Matopo few appear. The lines from the nose could depict bleeding in trance but animals may bleed from the nose in death.

7

Mind, Myth, Magic or Reality?

"These are messages from other cultures, other worlds, and we know nothing of the artists' original intentions or the transformations in meaning that the art has undergone, so there is no single correct interpretation. However, since it is better to light a candle than to curse the darkness, what one can do is to put forward observations, interpretations and hypotheses about the images, which can be evaluated and eventually discarded when something better comes along."

PAUL G. BAHN

There are hidden dangers in interpretation and the trap we fall into is to superimpose our own cultural standards upon the paintings. This problem may be surmountable but before embarking on the journey of discovery, a cautionary word! Differing interpretations abound, facts and surmises flow from amateurs and experts, but it is as well to remember that in the Matopo, firstly, archaeological findings are sparse and secondly, there is no oral history. Although hunter-gatherers have been extensively researched worldwide and we have a wealth of information to draw upon and parallels to make, we should follow the careful reasoning of the South African rock art specialist, David Lewis-Williams, who wrote in 1994 , "... it was recognised that the use of

This shape is unusual and inexplicable, appearing in association with the elliptical on p. 77.

Although they are many kilometres apart, this zoomorphic figure bears a great resemblance to that on p. 84.

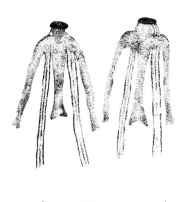

Although originally heavily painted, most images in this ground-level shelter are now faded, all else destroyed by termites, animals and humans. The termination of the torso and arms is shaped as the end of the 'trumpet' on p. 118. Any inter-pretation is speculative.

Bushman ethnography was fraught with many difficulties. Clearly, any game of ethnographic snap was impossible."[1]

In the Matopo the painted record is our primary source of information and with this limited factual knowledge the explanation of these images must necessarily remain speculative. One must tread warily for interpretation is a mine-field of hypotheses, many unearthed and carefully explored, some exploded and discarded, many waiting to be discovered and prised apart. As the whole arena of Bushmen art is open to speculation and many assumptions, it is hoped that the author will open up new avenues of thought and not trigger any explosive reactions with controversial theories!

We already know that over thousands of years Bushmen bands adapted to wide ranging environmental conditions and in so doing developed differing cultural forms. It could follow that in the Matopo a sub-culture may have arisen over a period of time, as evidenced by highly individualised painted images showing some similarities to the southern African paintings but many strong characteristic traits dissimilar to cultural trends to the north and south.

Believe it or Not

From time immemorial man has required the security and continuity of the religious ethic, the protection of some outside esoteric force, on which to rely and from which one draws courage to face the

Possibly linked heads, vertebrae, or a rattle. This image is sited on a long, low kopje in association with many other small painted sites where there is evidence of much Late Stone Age activity.

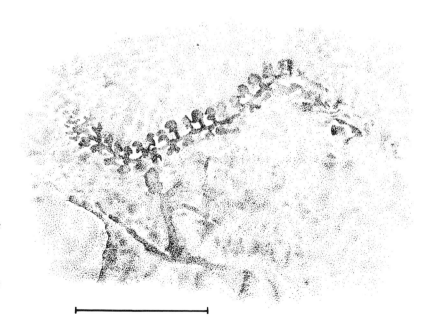

Although the lines from the face could be construed as bleeding from the nose in trance, there are no other indications that these figures are hallucinating; in fact, they walk in a determined and purposeful way.

This sinister figure, at 1.2m, is strikingly elongated and ghost-like in its appearance on the rock.

unknown. The Bushmen, living in a pre-scientific age surrounded by the inexplicable forces of the natural world, could also have looked for a sympathetic divine protection to explain happenings and conditions that could not be accounted for by reference to ordinary experience.

It is thought that the earliest religions evolved out of a concept that the body and soul, although separate entities, were not mutually exclusive and each was essential to the survival of the other. The soul was concerned with trance, hallucination and dreaming, and on departure of the soul the body died. This early religion is known as animism from the Latin *anima* meaning the soul. Unfairly, the prehistoric hunter-gatherer societies are pilloried as pagans for following this belief system, but as we hurtle towards our environmental doom, can we afford to condemn peoples that had learnt the art of living harmoniously with nature and respecting nature as their god?

It is known that animistic religions are selective, pliable and diverse and, as the psychologist Richard Katz points out, "The history of

The unreality of the attached bucks' heads deflects from the normality of the group scene. To emphasise this aspect there are lines from the nose, ears, armpits; extended fingers and pelvic emission. The head of the isolated, small antelope to the right and above is a mirror image of the buttocks attachment.

A zoomorphic figure showing some similarity to the image on p. 79. The only clear remaining painting on a rough exfoliated rock face. It is probable that the centre piece was white.

spiritual knowledge is an incessant struggle to tell its story in a way that is clear and accurate."[2] The art historian, E.H. Gombrich, was ahead of his time in realising that these aboriginal people had, "... uncanny powers of visualisation, their alleged grasp of the visible world unspoilt by the intervention of logic and the ravages of analytical reasoning."[3]

Present day Kalahari religious beliefs, which themselves have great variety, cannot be applied specifically to the Matopo paintings as much may have changed over 2 000 years.

Through the years we have been transported from a people reliant upon traditional beliefs, myths and magic, to our present day unemotional materialism. Two worlds so different, yet in man's passage through time, the hunter-gatherers are our closest relatives and could teach us the secret of survival.

To place ourselves back in the days of the Matopo Bushmen we must appreciate that people living in a pre-literate culture would have seen the world in a very different way and the complexity of their thought processes almost defy verbal interpretation (see pages 82/83).

The remains of an intriguing long lizard-like shape, clear for 71 cm and faded for another 76 cm. The central figure has mythical overtones.

Communications

The essence of religion is repetitive symbolism and each religion, with its accepted creed, is identifiable by its personal symbols, so can we assume that in the rock paintings we see repetitive icons associated with the Bushmen's beliefs, and that the repetition of imagery reinforced beliefs holding all the known and unknown world together with no dividing line between? This inter-relatedness between paintings and people would have supported the structure of their society, the fabric woven with tight communication skills to maintain the essential cohesiveness between the Bushmen themselves and their natural surroundings.

The art could be seen as a communication system following rules known by painter and audience alike, therefore enabling the messages to be easily read and understood while reinforcing deeply held beliefs and traditions. Due to the absence of the written word, the hunter-gatherers' life is one of intense verbal communication and continuous observation, this possibly being reinforced visually by the paintings, emphasising the significance of the subjects, objects and actions portrayed. Interpretation would then emerge holistically through the association and linking of the images. But, due to the fragmentary nature of the work that shows us only part of the complete story, we should take heed of the Art Professor Daniel M. Mendelowitz's words when he observed that a certain level of ambiguity demands creative participation to complete the meaning of the work. "The very act of imaginative involvement, operating in conjunction with the vague and

This scene holds an element of the sinister but this may be because of the images' likeness to the praying mantis and we know, as the Bushmen must have done, that the female mantis consumes its mate after copulation.

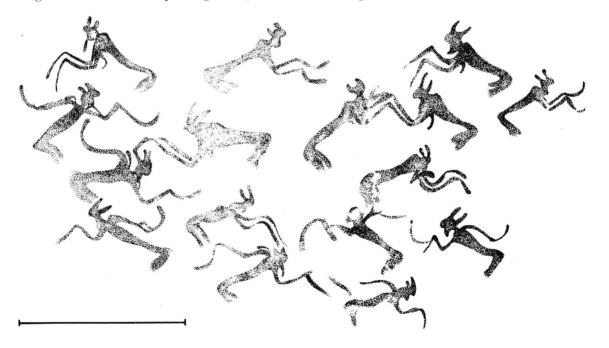

A scene showing certain images that appear repeatedly at other sites – the lying figures could be seen either as 'ecstatic' (as in trance) or merely at rest; the three grouped figures could illustrate the laying on of hands by a healer with the therianthropic shaman to the left. A degraded elliptical appears below. This is one of many sites in a densely painted area. Antelope, a therianthrope on all fours and a yellow mythical animal are painted on the same boulder.

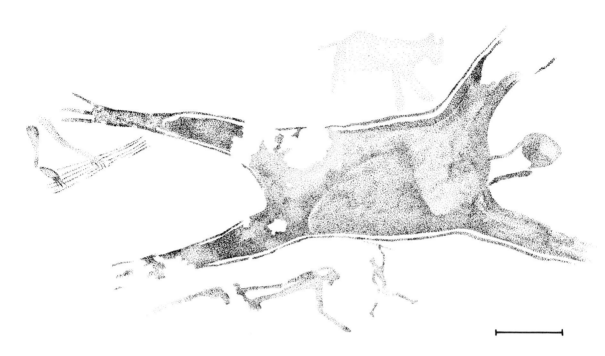

The site is small, the figure huge! The outline would seem to be important, as if separating the body from the spirit. Realistically, this could be a flayed karross.

This image is part of a well preserved composite scene, not shown, and is of interest for its similarity to that above.

undefined elements in the work, permits the viewer to interpret these undefined elements in terms most meaningful to himself ... permitting the viewer to see what he wants to see." [4]

Understanding the San rituals, their affinity with nature and close association with animals, may open the door to interpretation of the paintings, for the mind is its own place and the hunter-gatherers' mind was placed in nature.

Within the art there is a striking abundance of animals, especially mammals, and an important finding by Silberbauer in the Kalahari was that the San have, "... no concept of man's primacy as the most favoured amongst creatures. Instead, man has a place among them in a matrix of interdependent, interacting systems in which statuses are complementary rather than ranked." [5] This interdependence goes far beyond the people's normal need for meat. Humans take on animal forms, these therianthropic creatures appearing frequently in the Matopo paintings. The complexity of these unnatural images would seem to mean that the people had no sharp dividing line between animal and man. Silberbauer also found that the San God N!adima protected man and animals equally, this equality demanding respect for the animal and co-operation with nature that did not allow for the present day assumption of superiority by man; all life in its many varied forms was equally important. This god was not individualised, he appeared in many different guises and, to the hunter-gatherers, spirits could manifest themselves in nature. Universally, in aboriginal societies it is an accepted belief that trees, rocks and even water are inhabited by the gods.

Research in the Kalahari has found that the San saw the mammals as having knowledge and concepts allied to humans, but birds, insects and reptiles did not share the same exalted place in the hierarchy of human and animal.

Can we draw a parallel between the San and the Paviotso Indians of North America, researched by Joan Halifax, who believe that, "A long time ago, all the animals were Indians (they could talk)" and "that is why the animals help the people to be shamans."[6] In shamanistic cultures the world is seen in zoomorphic form. An extension of this belief places the animals as participants in the trance experience; psychologically bound to man.

We now distance ourselves from animals, a great deal of our empathy gone, using and manipulating them mercilessly to our own

The markings on the face give this figure a sable-like appearance. Possibly therianthropic, it has emanations from the nose and stomach. Little painting remains on this wall, the site hidden and difficult to find.

Here we are dealing in possibilities but if one uses the trance hypothesis, the lines portray sweat and exudations from orifices, and therefore an example of both man and animal in trance.

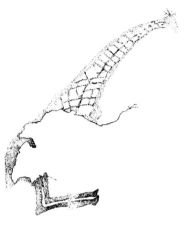

advantage. But once, as hunter-gatherers, we lived with them closely and successfully. We saw them in our fantasies and dreams, and integration was reality. In the Matopo paintings there is much evidence of this in the antelope and bird-men, humans with animal muzzles and cloven feet. The man became animal, the animal was the man.

Realistic scenes are few and portray only a limited aspect of daily life – men carrying bows and arrows and women with digging sticks – but little of domestic pursuits. No cooking and eating, few children, no domestic scenes, no love-making, no tanning of leather, no basket-making and no burials. The mundane routines are not shown, emphasising by their absence their relative insignificance.

The sun beats down unrelentingly on this painting and the exposure to changes in temperature may have caused the central exfoliation. The artists have drawn too many realistic giraffe for this human's seated posture not to be intentional. The main body of this animal has exfoliated away.

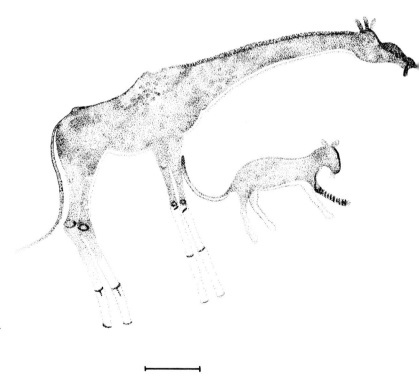

The use of white, ochre, and sienna appears almost decorative, akin to human body paint. The significance of the lines from both animals' noses could be seen as bleeding in trance. Alternatively, blood from the nose signifies the early stages of death.

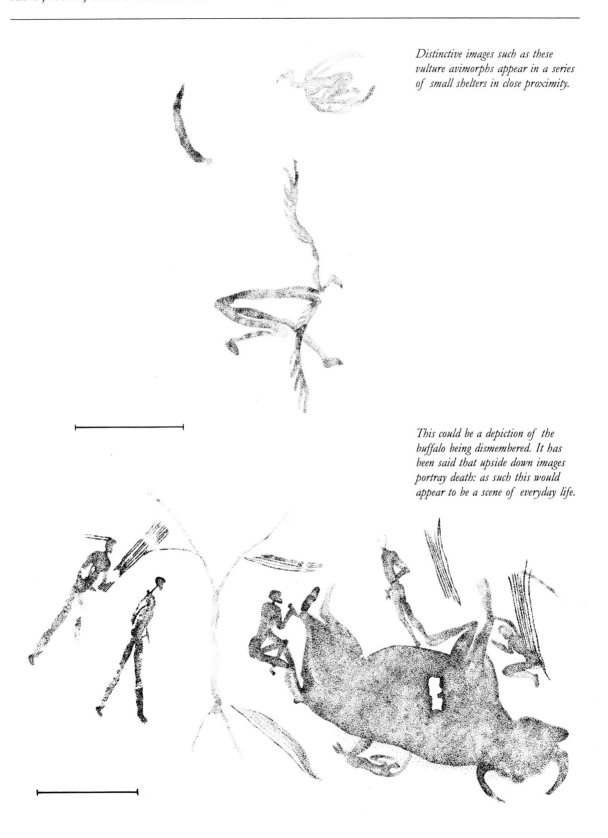

Distinctive images such as these vulture avimorphs appear in a series of small shelters in close proximity.

This could be a depiction of the buffalo being dismembered. It has been said that upside down images portray death: as such this would appear to be a scene of everyday life.

This illustration of what has, or has not, survived, an added complication in the task of interpretation, compounded by difficulties encountered when recording heavily over painted images (super-positioning). Even amongst the confusion one can see the white figures and ostrich head and legs.

Hallucination or Reality?

In South Africa where San oral history has been recorded, many of the paintings can be placed historically in the last few centuries and this has led to the trance-dance hypothesis. Here beliefs are focused on the evocative dance rituals used as a binding force to stabilise their society and provide a dynamic purpose to life. The dance is of vital importance, many taking part, the women clapping and singing, the dancers moving rhythmically, adopting stylised poses, sweating profusely and stamping their feet, at times bleeding from the nose and eventually falling into trance. Repetitive rhythms in crowd situations induce an altered state of consciousness and in this trance-like state the mind is released, allowing free-ranging hallucinatory experiences, the all important pivotal axis around which the San society revolved.

In hallucination there is perception of an object when no such object is present and still today, many people with finely tuned imaginations have normally occurring hallucinatory experiences which may unfortunately be seen as a mark of instability. One must bear in mind that an altered state of consciousness may also be induced by isolation, sleep deprivation and many other abnormal circumstances. Through the centuries man has been intrigued by hallucination, expanding the boundaries of the mind and offering a separate reality. It is of importance to understand that the nature of hallucination makes imagery and reality indistinguishable. Could this be the key to an holistic interpretation of the paintings, always remembering that we are dealing with possibilities?

Writing in *Ecstasy*, Marghanita Laski emphasises that these ecstatic experiences "... are to be valued not for the delight they give – which is great – but for their beneficial results. These results may be generally expressed as improved mental organisation, whether this takes the form of replacing uneasiness and dissatisfaction with ease and satisfaction, or of appearing to confirm a sought belief."[7] And this is borne out by research in the Kalahari where the exorcising dances leading to ecstatic episodes are used to dispel tensions and conflicts within the community. In some circles this has become the overriding approach to interpretation, and in the Matopo paintings there are many images that could be manipulated to fit this hypothesis when interpretation is controlled by cultural differences. An excellent example of this is given by Sir David Weatherall, Doctor and author at Oxford University who describes the African and southeast Asian practise of koro when males tie a rock to their penis in the belief that the organ is shrinking (see this page and page 94). This is accepted by the community as normal, but at Oxford would be seen as disturbed behaviour![8] Inevitably, interpretation is in the eye and mind of the

There is no recorded evidence of penis infibulation in recent Southern African hunter-gatherer societies but, with no ethnological record, we cannot say that this was not a practice used 2000 years ago in the Matopo.

*Certainly one of the most amazing
scenes in the book, if not in the
Matopo. The ecstatic dance of figures
is vibrant with meaning but difficult
to interpret.*

beholder and even the most straightforward images may be given fanciful constructs.

In whatever way the altered state of consciousness has been induced, these events have been used by aboriginal societies since time immemorial to reinforce cultural traditions, and at the very heart of these cosmic experiences, acting as the catalyst and energiser, stands the Shaman or healer as this figure is known in San culture.

Through the ages shamanistic experiences have been shown to possess great similarity, only between cultures the interpretation differs. Belief in these experiences lies in the trancer's ability to activate a spiritual potency which is seen as a radiating power emanating from his being and influencing the people, animals, hunting and every other facet in the complex interaction of spiritual and daily life.

Shamans are "... in communication with the world of gods and spirits. Their bodies can be left behind while they fly to unearthly realms. They are poets and singers. They dance and create works of art. They are not only spiritual leaders but also judges and politicians, the repositories of the knowledge of the culture's history, both sacred and secular. They are familiar with cosmic as well as physical geography; the ways of plants, animals, and the elements are known to them. They are psychologists, entertainers, and food finders. Above all, however, shamans are technicians of the sacred and masters of ecstasy."[9] (Halifax)

Unlike South Africa, dance scenes in the Matopo are sporadic, but are we seeing depictions of the varied and numerous manifestations of trance? If trancing was overwhelmingly important, how was it

These figures appear on a wall 7m long, originally heavily painted but now only staining and fragmented paint remain. The two figures on the right are unusual for the combination of gender, skirts, long whisks and karros cloak. The temptation is to see them as female shamans. On the other side of the valley appears one of the most unusual scenes in the Matopo (p. 94) and it is difficult not to connect the two.

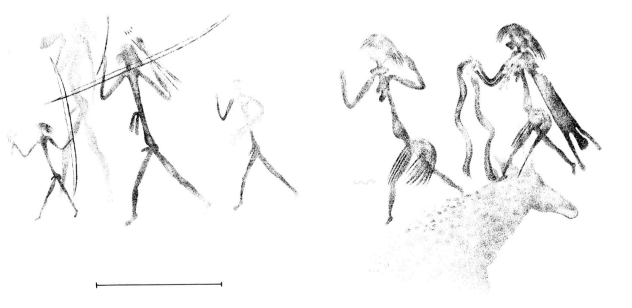

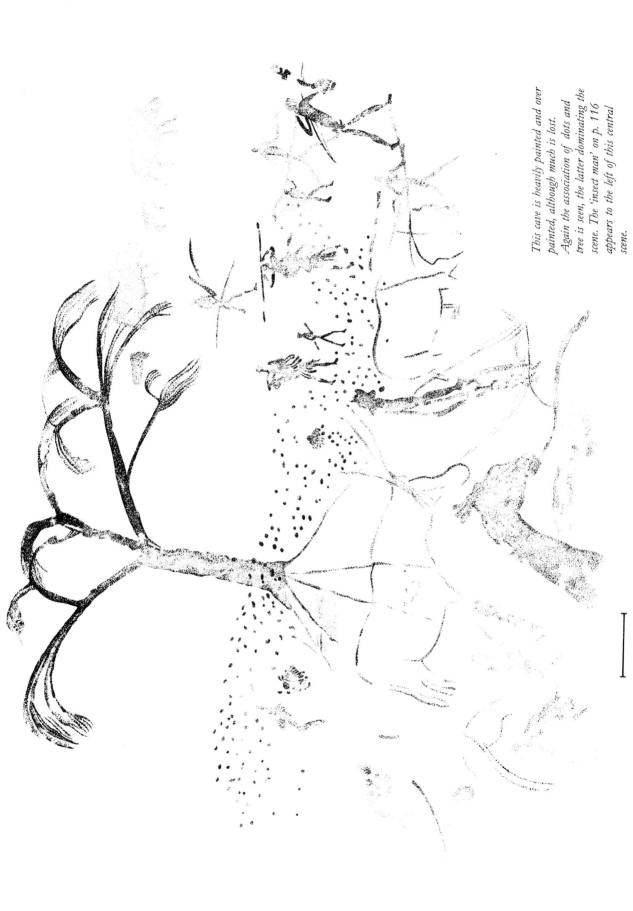

This cave is heavily painted and over painted, although much is lost. Again the association of dots and tree is seen, the latter dominating the scene. The 'insect man' on p. 116 appears to the left of this central scene.

achieved? Here we enter the realms of informed guesswork supported by possible evidence in the paintings, the Matopo environment and worldwide historical facts.

Let us first look at our 'New Age' society today, for it would seem that not only now but eternally, human beings have been seeking an "artificial paradise"! Escape from reality in discos with flashing lights and drumming music helps some to the temporary shelter of another world, and psychoactive substances, so widely used and abused, provide an escape route to ecstasy.

Aldous Huxley investigated and experimented with hallucinogenic drugs in the earlier part of this century and wrote in *The Doors of Perception*, "All the vegetable sedatives, narcotics, all the euphorics that grow on trees, the hallucinogens that ripen in berries or can be squeezed from roots – all, without exception, have been known and systematically used by human beings from time immemorial."[10] and so it is in the Matopo with its endless, prolific and diverse flora, some known to be hallucinogens which surely the Bushmen knew and could have used.[11]

A fire-blackened and exfoliated shelter. The images appear in association with animals and hunters and would seem to be a type of vegetation.

This is one of the few dance scenes in the Matopo and may be connected with the mythical 'Hippo Hunt' on p. 119; the two sites being in close association. The armbands are unusual, and the pattern resembles the three objects – possibly bags – that lie above. There appears to be a long 'scarf' intwined between the arms of the central dancers.

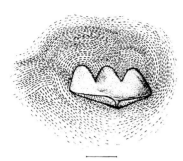

This form approximates the main scene which appears on p. 66/67 and is painted in burnt sienna with orangey ochre infill. The flecks are not at random, the pattern very precise.

Aldous Huxley, during his experiments with mescalin, obtained from the American cactus Peyote, the precursor of LSD, frequently saw two-dimensional hallucinatory images and on one occasion saw that the, "Table, chair and desk came together in a composition that was like something by Braque or Juan Gris, a still-life recognisably related to the objective world, but rendered without depth, without any attempt at photographic realism."[12] An important parallel is immediately seen in the Matopo art, for Huxley's hallucinations are two dimensional and conceptual – as the Bushmen artists painted.

For the Bushmen the variety of symbols was unequivocally understood, but we stand before the rocks, distanced by time and culture and confused by the mysterious complexities of strange images. Can we interpret these signs and their significance?

Does this show an emphasis on the tree in association with humans? Are these figures possible trance manifestations with pin heads and altered body shape? The tree could then indicate the use of hallucinogenic drugs.

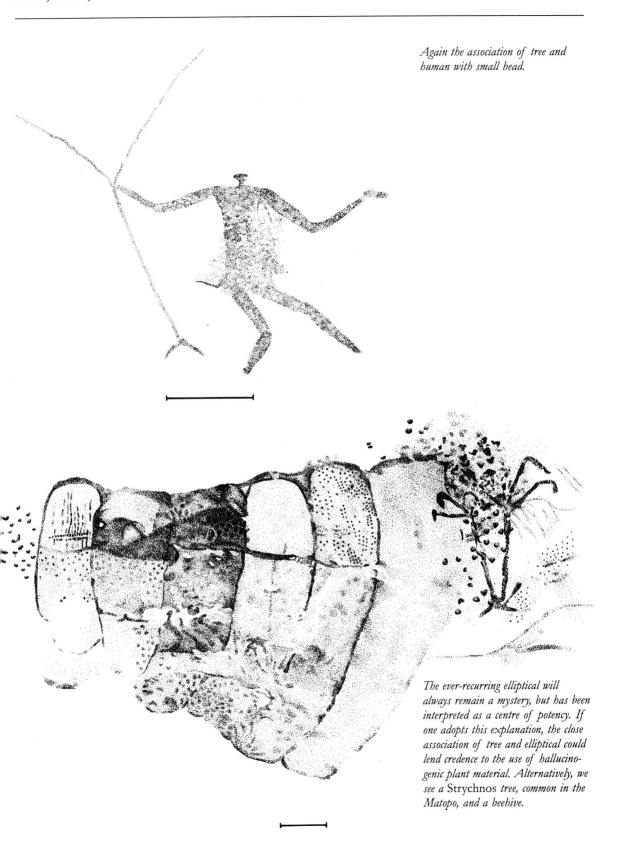

Again the association of tree and human with small head.

The ever-recurring elliptical will always remain a mystery, but has been interpreted as a centre of potency. If one adopts this explanation, the close association of tree and elliptical could lend credence to the use of hallucinogenic plant material. Alternatively, we see a Strychnos *tree, common in the Matopo, and a beehive.*

Facing south in a very high, small shelter, these paintings are of startling clarity and great artistic ability. But they do not seem to portray everyday life. Whether it is myth, dream, fantasy or hallucination, we will never know.

The swollen belly (on a male figure) and fringed face are unusual. The long line from the hand meanders and disappears across the rock, connecting to a very faded similar figure.

The Signs and their Significance

Our mental imagery is rich and varied and the complexities of these abstractions could be mirrored, if not matched exactly, by that of our hunter-gatherer ancestors. Trancing and hallucination are in keeping with the present day obsession for psychological phenomena, but a blanket approach should not be applied indiscriminately to all Zimbabwean rock art.

In today's world, the philosopher Wade Savage discusses the inter-relatedness of these mental processes suggesting that, "... it would surely be beneficial to psychological research to assume that sensing, perceiving, hallucinating, dreaming, fantasising, and thinking cannot be understood in isolation from one another."[13] and we can use these present day assumptions in attempting a reconstruction of the hunter-gatherer's thought processes.

Through the ages, across cultures and in geographically remote areas around the globe, hallucinations are experienced in dramatically similar stages of fantasy. Whether a member of the northern Siberian Yakut tribe or a drug taker on the streets of London, almost an exact progression of imagery is experienced although always very differently culturally conditioned and controlled. Can we assume that the Bushmen (remember: our biological and psychological equals) would have experienced similar stages of imagery?

During and after hallucination perception is enhanced, the imagination expands, accompanied by a feeling of self-revelation and a clarity of vision, suddenly – "the world is one's oyster"! Throughout the experience, descriptive symbols such as words or pictures can be precisely defined and their controlled use communicated to others, and there is the important ability of clear recall on the return to normality which could have enabled the Bushman to transpose his

In the past the head attachments have been identified as arrows in a headband, but may be head adornment. Head-dress and penis attachments may have a deeper meaning and communicate an unknown message.

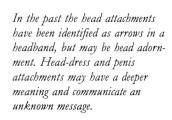

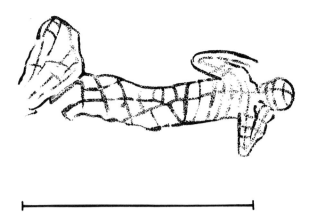

trance experiences onto the rocks, reinforcing the integration of these unreal images into the reality of daily life. It is of interest that during the course of research, artists have reported to the author an improved creativity after the use of hallucinogenic drugs.

Universally, from whatever creed or culture, as the hallucination transforms the mind, geometric designs explode across the 'screen', gradually forming into known cultural and environmental icons, these images directly projected onto and amalgamating with the geometry of lines, dots, cones and spirals. For modern man, the computer, fax and plastic rubble, the "cultural necessities", may float across the picture. In prehistoric man, the specks, flecks and lines, seen in the paintings, would have been culturally conditioned to form the animals, hunters, mystical creatures and the many other forms. This imagery reflects people's deep association with the natural world, and for the Bushmen, the trancers' hallucinatory experiences may have formed a mystical religious cult which, like all religions, provided an anchor of repeated imagery in a world of fluctuating hopes and despairs.

Elliptical Images

Elliptical images in varying shapes appear constantly in the Matopo paintings and are closely associated with large and small dots, short flecks, longer broken lines and octagonal honeycomb shapes. These are contained not only within the elliptical forms, but flowing in, away and around, touching, enveloping and entering other images of humans, animals or plants. It has been postulated that these icons are centres of metaphysical power from which potency emanates. Solid lines connecting images are thought to be a pathway for transmission of potency between humans, animals, trees and mythical creatures, and evidence of the shaman's/healer's power to control and manipulate

It is of interest to compare Cran Cooke's painting of this scene as it appears in The Rock Art of Central Africa, *pp. 126/127, with our copy. The finer details were left out, early researchers not realizing the importance of analysing the scene holistically. The buck-headed snake and associated mythical animal have a similarity to those appearing on p. 7.*

by merging the tangible and intangible worlds. While one would not wish to refute any possible theories it is unwise to adopt too narrow and dogmatic a view where there is no possible ethnological reference.

Alternatively, and it is quite probable, we are seeing bees entering and leaving honey combs. To the Bushmen the octagonal honeycomb shape, possibly seen in the first stages of trance, could emphasise the known importance of bees. Controlled by cultural association, the trancer's mind could transpose lines and curves to shape the honeycomb associated with the supernatural powers of bees and honey. In an altered state of consciousness constant background humming may be heard and it is not beyond the bounds of credulity that this further emphasised the significance of bees in the Bushmen's mind. Even today honey is venerated, and Laurens van der Post, in close contact with Bushmen through youth and adolescence, knew that, "Like primitive peoples the world over, Bushman had a honey mystique. Honey was not merely a physical substance but an image evoking great creative energies in his life ... [and] honey, in the basic imagery of man, was a symbol of wisdom. It is so with the Bushman;

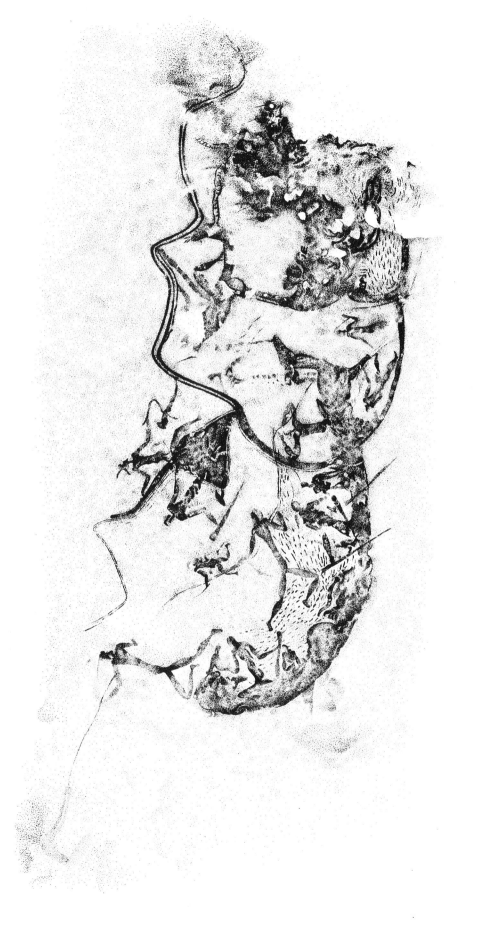

Angulated double lines appear, encapsulating many active human figures and one antelope. The painting originally continued to the right and left so we are again looking a fragmentary remains of a greater story. A striking example of the difficulties in interpretation.

Although one could interpret this large image as a centre of potency, it could equally be seen as a bulbous root or fruit of nutritional import-ance. This painting is placed to the right of Pager's 'bee smoking' scene (below) and therefore could represent the trunk of a tree, the bees within, and escaping above as the people smoke them out.

This well known painting has been much discussed and copied over the years. Harald Pager interpreted the images as the smoking of a bees' nest. The elliptical form corresponds to the many others illustrated and the flecks inside and streaming away have been interpreted as specks of potency.

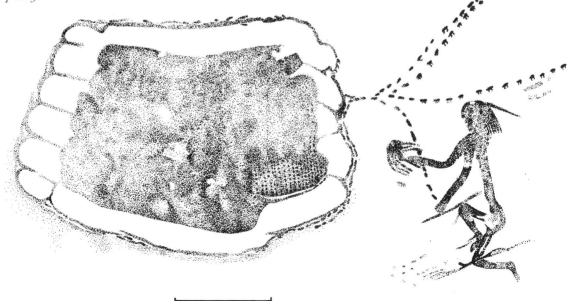

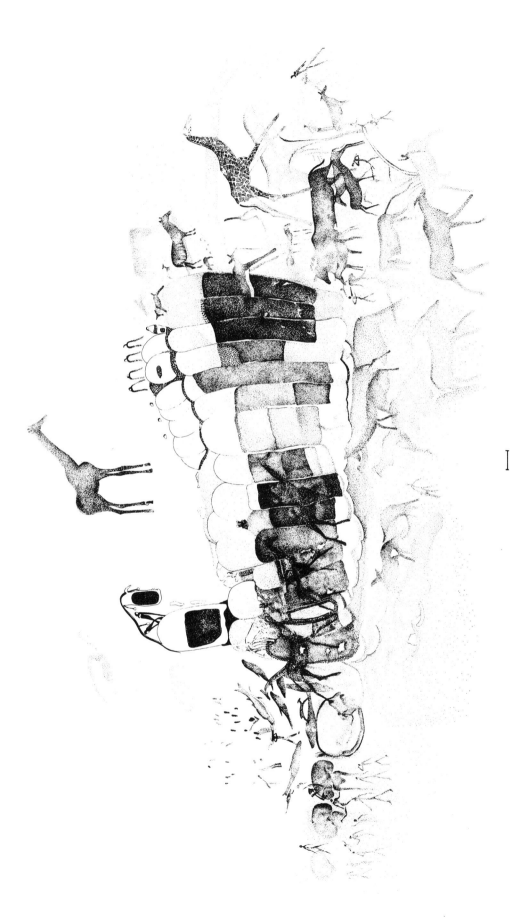

Located in Nanke Cave this is the largest and most beautiful of the ellipticals, closely associated with many giraffe and clearly defined fish. Again interpretation ranges from "centres of potency" (Garlake, The Hunters Vison, Plate XXIV) to a "landscape of the surrounding hills" or a "bee hive".

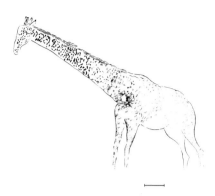

This giraffe, coloured dark purple with a strong outline and distinctive spots, appears below and in close association with the scene on p. 55.

it is so with many other primitive peoples I know."[14] Honey and wisdom, specks and bees, lines and potency – an interlinking matrix of meaning, unravelling across the rocks. Today the complexity of the potency theory is more appealing, the reality of bees old fashioned and simplistic, one cannot say which, if either, is correct.

The artist was a master of observation, drawing animals with sympathetic realism, but some of the animals so closely associated with ellipticals have a sense of unreality. The spotted cats, leopard and cheetah, and the giraffe appear as icons of apparent importance painted in association with the elliptical forms. It is possibly a coincidence that their markings relate to the so called spots of trance imagery and that the lion, hyena and jackal, with no obvious markings, are noticeable by their absence!

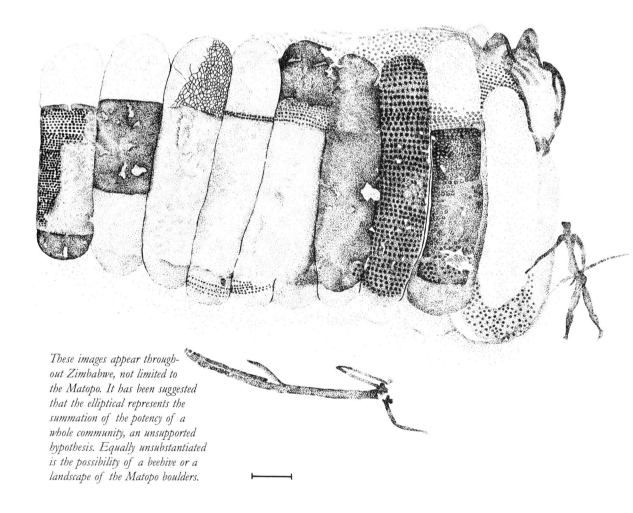

These images appear throughout Zimbabwe, not limited to the Matopo. It has been suggested that the elliptical represents the summation of the potency of a whole community, an unsupported hypothesis. Equally unsubstantiated is the possibility of a beehive or a landscape of the Matopo boulders.

Mythical Creatures

An enigma to ourselves, but one can assume that to the Bushmen, known and recognisable symbols, mythical creatures, by combining the differing characteristics of separate animals, emphasise a symbiotic relationship. Interpretation is tenuous and any attempts to analyse these imaginary beings as 'rain animals' in the light of present day Bushmen ethnology steps into the unacceptable realm of wild supposition.

In the Maleme valley, hidden in a dark, boulder-strewn cave, are mystical giant creatures, part bird, giraffe and human. Unique and unfathomable, these figures have in the past been seen as birds – for Cran Cooke, the Whale-headed Stork and, for Nick Walker, the site of boys' puberty rites! But the true interpretation may never be known. Far to the east and high above the great canyon of the Mtshabezi valley, similar long legged giant 'birds' present us with another mystery (see below). The many other enigmatic images seen in the Matopo may be the products of myths or hallucinations or the imagination.

This mermaid-like image may represent a myth or trance experience but the local people refer to these one-legged figures as isotokwane, *a portent of evil. Several small shelters in the immediate vicinity have very unusual images not recorded elsewhere in the Matopo.*

Traces of paint show that this large cave must have been extensively painted. The 'birds' are placed very high, escaping the worst of the prevailing weather which impacts directly into the site. Interpretation is impossible but in their large size and shape they bear a resemblance to the images located centrally in the National Park and described by Cooke as 'whale headed storks' and by Walker as the site of boys' puberty rites.

The Snake

Since the dawn of history, 20 to 30 000 years ago, humans have been painting snake images on the walls of shelters and caves. Ancient and modern hunter-gatherer societies have seen the snake as possessing supernatural power. Anatomically, so far removed from people and other animals, so swift yet legless, so different and dangerous, the snake is revered and reviled.

In the Matopo the Bushmen also recognised and acknowledged its unique and fascinating form, possibly elevating the snake to a place of veneration. Here, in the paintings, the snake assumes a status of importance by virtue of its great size and appears unrealistically horned, two-headed or buck-headed. The snake, by shedding its skin, is associated with the ancient belief of achieving eternal youth and immortality. This ability to slough the skin sets the snake apart from mammals but brings it closer to the shaman/healer who also has the ability to metamorphose – one in reality, the other symbolically. Is it possible that during trance the potency of the snake and shaman, two powerful beings, is interwoven?

This mythical snake, often much larger than life, is painted in close

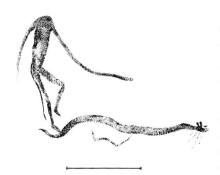

The long arm and tail of this therianthropic being mimic the snake.

*In a small and secluded shelter the
antelope illustrates the close
association of human and animal as
is seen with the Gulubahwe Snake
(pp. 112/113). The remains of a
very faded elliptical form lies centrally
between the two scenes.*

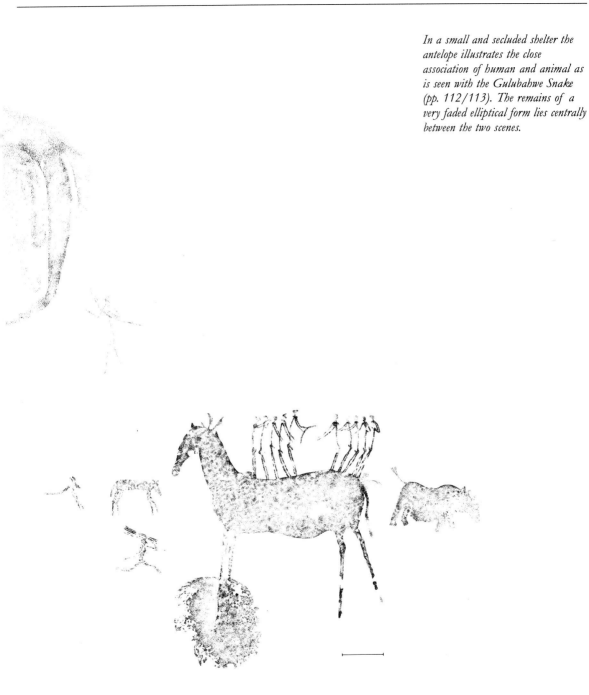

The 5m long snake, in Gulubahwe
Cave, is one of two within 12km
and both show the close proximity of
man, antelope and reptile. The small,
sitting buck, above, appears
repeatedly in large and small sites,
almost as if a signature. The solid
infill on the far left may be the
remains of the image with swanlike
head that also appears in Nanke
and Buhwe Caves.

proximity to people and animals, negating a threat and suggesting a beneficial relationship. The image may represent a deep need to appease, placate and establish a harmonious relationship between man and snake. The broken lines may represent potency connecting the images. Could we be seeing the shaman/healer in transition through the snake, harnessing and utilising the serpent's power to guide and assist the people and animals?

Here we venture into the realms of wild hypotheses, but it has also been postulated that the undulating snake's back represents the surrounding 'waves' of hills peopled with animals and humans.

Alites

The flying forms, half human and bird, have to be creatures of the mind. The human yearning for escape by elimination of gravity, and achieving a feeling of buoyancy, seem part of the human psyche.

The known and accepted experience during hallucination of apparent levitation, the ability for out of body travel and transportation to another world, could explain the flying forms. In mystical flight of magical transcendence there is a universal belief that shamans achieve this release of the soul.

After taking a hallucinogenic drug in South America the ethnobotanist, Wade Davis, felt as if, "caught on the wings of birds, passing through space ... flying along the wild face of mountains, in the wind the touch of clouds on feathers ... the wind carrying us away into the night sky and beyond the scattered start."
(One River, Wade David, p. 452). A delightful interpretation but this figure could as easily be part of a mythical story.

Dreams

Our distance in time and culture from the Bushmen is so great that we are striving against almost impossible barriers of conception to arrive at the essence of meaning and a dawn of understanding. To awake from dreams and see the imagery as reality is not our way. To day-dream and acknowledge the experience as true life, is not acceptable and for us the hallucination cannot be a reality, but for the Bushmen there appears to have been an important relationship between the mind and the painted image, and in moving towards an appreciation and acceptance of this ability to integrate the two worlds, it is necessary to understand, as the philosopher, Sebastian Gardner says, "... the underlying nature of the experience of painting lies in the fact that paintings give us experiences of absent or non-existent objects. Now this is something that occurs also in dreams, daydreams, and hallucination."[15]

In dreams and hallucinations similar and recurring images infiltrate both experiences, but where is the dividing line? The psychology of dreams tells us much of the dreamer's culture/life-style. In the 1940s, the German geologists Henno Martin and Hermann Korn, having

The two main figures are unsexed,
the faces and long hair with crown
and antennae seem insect-like but the
hunting equipment emphasises a
hunter's role. The clearly painted
single arrow sign is inexplicable and
points to the small figure super-
imposed on the larger. The heads
show definite facial features which are
seldom found in the art.

spent some time in voluntary isolation in the Namib desert, once populated by hunter-gatherers, noticed a change in the subjects of their dreams: "Animals began to play an increasing part in them and the distinction between human beings and animals became blurred. There seemed to be no particular mystery about this; after all, for a couple of years now our whole life had revolved around them; they were our fellow beings and our existence depended largely on them. Supposing we had led such a life not merely for a couple of years, but from childhood onwards! How natural such dreams would be! Perhaps this was the origin of mythology – to be found in the heritage of all peoples – in which human beings and animals mingle and merge into each other."[16] Are these the therianthropes of the paintings peopling the Bushmen's world in waking, dreaming or trancing? A mystical world glimpsed by the solitary Germans but elusive to our comprehension.

This anthropomorphic being is quite unique in the author's experience and found in association with the scene on p. 96.

Manifestations of Trance?

A unique and fascinating feature in the human imagery centres on the apparent extension of bodily matter, unnaturally lengthened arms and long pointed fingers, the body stretched beyond physiological limits. These sensations are described today during trance and hallucination and could explain the intriguing augmentation of the body, and parallels

These extended therianthropic figures have hooved back feet, lengthened arms, lines from the armpits and orifices and elongated fingers. They lean towards the remains of an elliptical form. An amazing line of 600 Impala are painted through the cave, connecting the main scenes.

Here we see, in Bambata Cave, a particular emphasis on long fingers, with the arms above the head, attitudes that could be used to explain a trance sensation. Other images from this large cave appear on p. 108.

in interpretation could be drawn between the present day experiences of spirit mediums and the hunter-gatherers. These aboriginal people could have undergone similar trance-like experiences showing a striking likeness to those of the modern medium.

In trance, today's spirit medium is said to exude an amorphous, viscous substance. This nebulous 'ectoplasmic' fluid comes from any part of the body, but generally from the natural orifices[17] and is seen to metamorphose into known cultural symbols as experienced in hallucination. Earlier this century a psychologist/physician, Dr V. Gustave Geley, investigated metaphysical phenomena and describes, "This manifestation is a premonitory phenomenon, ... The substance itself emanates from the whole body of the medium, but especially from the natural orifices and the extremities, from the top of the head, from the breasts, and the tips of the fingers."[18] In the Matopo paintings an extended 'neck' culminating in an antelope head appears from buttocks and penis; lines emerge from ears and female figures are seen with legs parted and a vaginal emission. The nose extends dramatically, stretching beyond the body, sometimes touching the ground and bifurcating at the end. A verbal description has been given to the author of nose extension while using a psychedelic substance, the nose growing away across the room to be reeled in manually by the shocked hallucinator!

In the paintings the human image with extended nose has been described over the years, as a trumpet or alpine stock but no other musical instruments appear in the paintings, not even the drum, historically so closely allied to inducing a state of exaltation. But the

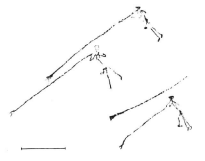

Solitary 'trumpeters' with emphasised penises drawn on an exposed unsheltered wall.

Three 'trumpeters' striding purposefully across the rock.

reality may be closer to the instrument used by the Pygmies of the Ituri forest in Uganda who fashion a trumpet out of hollowed wood. The instrument is central to their hunting beliefs and represents to them the voice of the forest in which they live.[19]

Consciousness is altered by whatever means and the mind plays very convincing tricks, easily believable in the Bushmen's world of largely unexplained phenomena.

A single, clear 'trumpeter' image painted on a long sloping wall, with two worked stone slabs in the shelter. This image appears at widely separated sites.

Agents of Information

Our Bushman of long ago, the hunter of dreams and reality, walks and runs across the rocks, carrying his quiver of arrows and delicately portrayed bow. "This image of arrow and bow lay deep in the Bushman's mind. It was the first instrument of his own fashioning which enabled him to apply his will at great distances from himself. All that I know of him suggests quite clearly that it was not merely an instrument for obtaining food but also a creation of the spirit to him."[20] (van der Post)

Traditional hunting scenes occur, but all is not quite what it seems, for many images are touched with unreality. The archer shoots towards the heavens or aims at flying human forms, the arrow heads emphasised and over-expanded, quite impractical for killing. Could this be the hunter symbolically touching all with the magic arrows of his power. Are these the arrows of 'death' – the symbolic death of the body in trance releasing the flying spirit to out of body travel?

In present day San communities the medicine man or healer plays

The extra legs and head could be an attempt to show movement or a superpositioning of one animal upon the other, an approach which is unique in the author's experience. The mythical, distorted figures, to the right, defy interpretation.

*Real or unreal, death or levitation or
an unknown myth explored?
Hallucination and an out of body
experience? A puzzling enigma?*

*Facing west, on a separate boulder,
at the same height as this scene is*
the dance *that appears on p. 97
and it may be that the two are
linked. This could be seen as a
realistic hippo hunt but the crouching
archer is using an unrealistic arrow
and it is as if the unwilling hippo is
being pushed and pulled. We see only
the small remains of the original
paintings, now being eaten by lichen.*

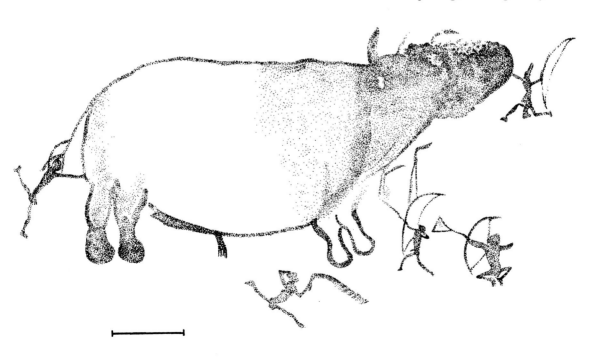

Several separate scenes in a fire-
blackened shelter. The realism of the
hunters is offset by the unknown
image to the left and the extended
'nose' or 'trumpet' held aloft by a
small figure. Expanded arrow heads
appear again.

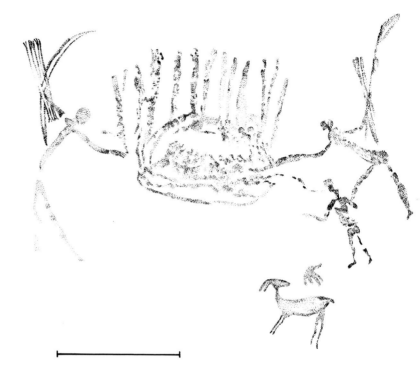

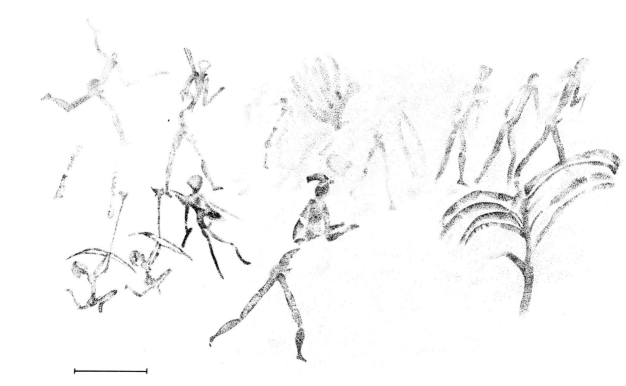

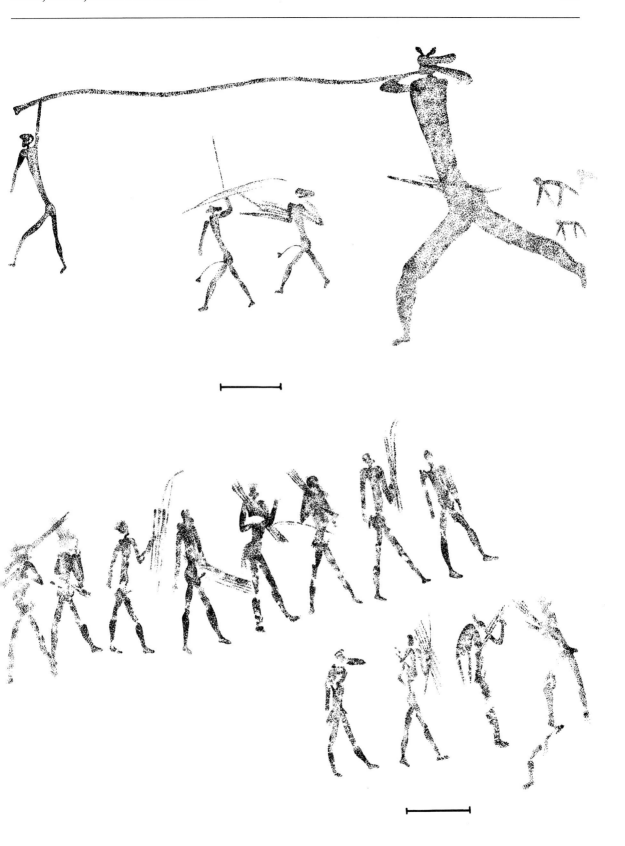

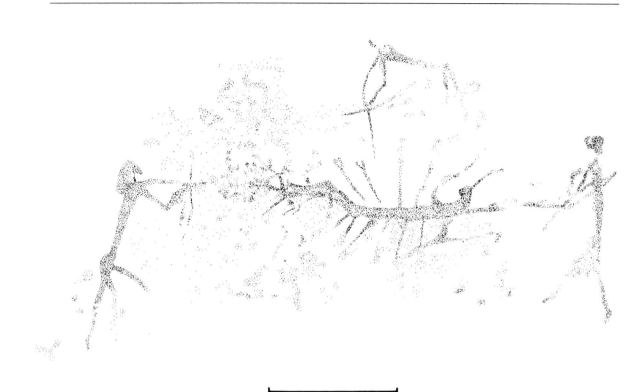

The access to this cave is difficult and dangerous. The rock face, unusually multicoloured, presents spectacular contrasts. The small group of paintings in the deepest recess are very faded and interpretation is difficult. Realistically, this could be a murder scene but the arrows might be instilling potency and the reclining figure transforming into an animal.

It would seem that there was another figure lying to the right and all the few paintings are isolated on a small area of rock, not part of a larger scene. The stance suggests a possible laying on of hands by the healer?

This indecipherable form with swan-like neck appears repeatedly in Nanke Cave and at other major sites. The close association with a 'trumpeter' may be coincidental. Nanke is renowned for its exquisite artwork.

an important role in the society. They speak of the arrows of healing piercing the body. These metaphoric arrows are associated with a prickling sensation, feeling like many thorns. Is there a parallel in the paintings: humans and animals transfixed by a multitude of arrows symbolic of healing, or is this murder in the Matopo? (see page 122).

It would seem that possibly the healer's role was important, and there are apparent scenes of healing by 'laying on of hands', (page 122) the power of the healer eliminating sickness and making the body whole. The psychological and physical implications of bodily contact, although under-valued in present day western society, seem to have been of inestimable importance to early hunter-gatherer societies. In the Kalahari, during the trance dance, the healer rubs his own sweat onto the one being healed, as sweat is regarded as a vital element in the healing process, a visible expression of the power contained within the healer.

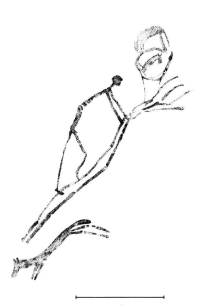

Is this a mythical story or just a man climbing a tree?

The Tree of Life

The tree, for most of us, has a special place in our imaginations for it symbolises union between the earth and the heavens – fed from above and below, earthbound but eternally reaching to the sky, as humans look to the heavens for cosmic help and strength.

Vegetation is virtually absent from the South African imagery but, conversely, trees and bushes in close proximity to people and animals appear in over 40 painted sites known to the author in the Matopo. The vegetation is non-specific – the 'leaves' painted as dots, dashes or broken lines. People and animals move within the branches and between trees (see page 2).

The natural cycles of nature, of dying and regrowth, may have been seen as a parallel with 'dying' in trance and a rejuvenated return, and the tree, the trancer and the snake share this startling ability of apparent regeneration which, for a people devoid of scientific explanations, could have been seen as dramatic and mysterious events.

In the Matopo the elephant appears noticeably less often than further north. Painted repetitively, kudu, tsessebe and sable assume a status of importance. Long lines of impala graze peacefully across the rocks (see page 116) and on occasion smaller antelope appear. Warthogs, bushpigs, baboons, zebras and jackals, all we see today they saw before us, and painted with great accuracy and feeling.

Analysis of images in the large caves would suggest that these were places of ritual meeting. In these caves, throughout the Matopo, are repeated the large elliptical forms, great snakes and interwoven lines, recognised and acknowledged within the Bushmen's world. Strange and unique images in the smaller sites show an individuality, as though they are the experiences of a single person, possibly only understood by the clan that used the shelter.

These painted rocks are a visual picture of the Matopo Bushmen's life, the people's concepts of supernatural forces merged with the daily life of man and animal; yet we may never know the whole meaning of the enigmatic drawings, the individual symbols or the relationship between each painted image. It is tempting to visualise a centuries old artistic tradition with successive generations maintaining cultural beliefs amongst a tolerant and easy going society.

Although interpretation is fraught with difficulties we are struck by the beauty and simplicity of the painting. One of the most experienced and well known rock art specialists, Paul Bahn, sees this aesthetic value in much prehistoric art and points out that, "One important criterion seems to be simplicity. Many of the works that we admire convey their impression with great economy of means."[21] The enigma of a complex culture revealed in a concise, controlled, and sophisticated artistic style.

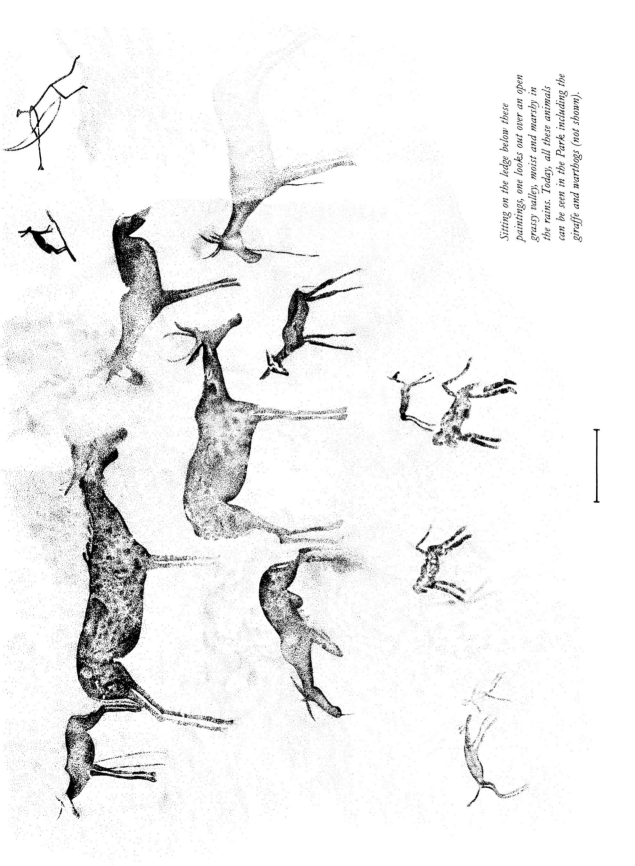

Sitting on the ledge below these paintings, one looks out over an open grassy valley, moist and marshy in the rains. Today, all these animals can be seen in the Park including the giraffe and warthogs (not shown).

... And Now, the Future

"Confronted with the necessities of economic development, and with the investments and jobs that are at stake, the preservation of rock art too often takes second place, whether in industrialised countries or not."

JEAN CLOTTES

Zimbabwe may have more than 30 000 rock art sites and the Matopo would seem to be the most densely painted, yet, as Pascall Taruvinga, Curator of Rock Art at the Museum of Human Sciences, Harare, points out, "It is pathetic that out of the estimated 30 000 sites only 15.3 % have been recorded."[1] But recording must proceed hand in hand with other disciplines in the field of rock art.

Interpretation, whilst recently making great advances and providing fascinating insights to the Bushmen's life, is not enough, as only concerted effort and awareness in conservation and preservation will retain this legacy for future generations.

Jean Clottes, as President of the International Committee on Rock Art, singles out the importance of protection emphasising that, "Rock art constitutes one of the essential components of humanity's cultural and religious heritage and it possesses a universal value."[2]

This book is the story of the Matopo Bushmen, long gone but remembered in their paintings. The story of a magic journey of discovery for the author, but written only to encourage care, appreciation and conservation of this priceless heritage.

"For us, the cave paintings re-create the hunter's way of life as a glimpse of history; we look through them into the past. But for the hunter, I suggest, they were a peep-hole into the future; he looked ahead. In either direction, the cave paintings act as a kind of telescope tube of the imagination: they direct the mind from what is seen to what can be inferred or conjectured."

JACOB BRONOWSKI

Bibliography

Preface (pp. v–viii)

Opening Quote: BACON Francis – *The Advancement of Learning and The New Atlantis*. Henry Frowde, Oxford University Press, p. 38.

1. RANSFORD O.N. – *Bulawayo: Historic Battleground of Rhodesia*, A.A. Balkema, Cape Town, 1968, p. 164.

Chapter 1: Preservation (pp. 1–8)

Opening quote: STEEL R. – As quoted by H.C. Woodhouse, Closing address, SARARA Conference, Drakensberg SA, Aug 1991

1. MENNELL F.P. – "Some aspects of the Matopos" – 2nd paper – *Proceedings of the Rhodesia Scientific Association, vol. vii Part II*, Aug 1908, p. 9.
2. GENGE P. – "Bravo Bednarik" *Pictogram*, SARARA, Vol. 3 No. 2. p. 18
3. BEDNARIK R.G. – "Rock Art Researchers as Rock Art Vandals" SARARA, Vol. 4, 1991, pp. 166–68.
4. GALE F. & JACOBS J. – "Aboriginal Art – Australia's Neglected Inheritance" *World Archaeology*, no. 19, 1987, pp. 226–235.
5. LOUBSER J. – "The conservation of rock engravings and rock paintings: removals to museums or selected exhibitions in the field?" *SA Journal of Science*, Vol. 90, Aug/Sept 9 1994, p. 456.
6. MEIKELJOHN K.I. – "The Deterioration and Preservation of Rock Art in the Kwazulu/Natal Clarens Formation", *Pictogram*, SARARA, Vol. 8 No. 1, July 1995. p. 4.
7. LE MAITRE S. – "The Rock Paintings of Quebec", INORA, No. 11, 1995, p. 24.
8. LOUBSER J. – "The conservation of rock engravings and rock paintings: removals to museums or selected exhibitions in the field?" *South African Journal of Science*, Vol. 90, Aug/Sept 1994, p. 455.
9. REED H. – *Art and Society*, Faber and Faber, London, 1967, p. 7

Chapter 2: Dating (pp. 9–13)

Opening Quote: BRODRICK A.H. – *Early Man – A Survey of Human Origins*, Hutchinson, London, 1948, p. 252

1. COOKE C.K. – *Rock Art of Southern Africa*, Books of Africa, Cape Town, 1969, p. 46.
2. BEDNARIK R.G. – INORA, No. 11, 1995, p. 10.
3. BEDNARIK R.G. – *Pictogram*, "About radiocarbon dating in palaeoart studies." Vol. 8, No. 1 July 1995, p. 16.
4. WATCHMAN A. – "Dating potential of the Foz Côa engravings." Unpublished report to the Electricidade de Portugal, 30 March 1995.
5. WALKER N.J. – *Late Pleistocene and Holocene Hunter-gatherers of the Matopos* (Doctoral thesis), Societas Archaeologica Upsaliensis, Uppsala, 1995

Chapter 3: And in the beginning (pp. 15–31)

Opening Quote: SCHOEMAN P.J. – *Hunters of the Desert Land*, Howard Timmins, Cape Town, 1961, p. 145.

1. KRÜGER J.S. – *Along Edges*, University of South Africa, Pretoria, 1995, p. 154.

2.   KONNER M. – "The Stone-Age Diet: Cuisine Sauvage" *The Sciences*, Sept/Oct 1985, p. 287.
3.   HALL R.N. – "Antiquity of the Bushman Occupation of Rhodesia" *Proceedings of the Rhodesia Scientific Association*, 1912, p. 143.
     DART R.A. – Foreword to *Ndedema* [H. Pager], Akademische Druck-u Verlagsanstalt, Austria. 1971, p. ix.
     TOBIAS P.V. (ed.) – *The Bushmen*, Human & Rousseau, Cape Town, 1978, p. 4.
4.   GARLAKE P.G. – *The Hunter's Vision*, British Museum Press and Zimbabwe Publishing House, 1995, p. 7.
5.   WALKER N.J. – *Late Pleistocene and Holocene Hunter-gatherers of the Matopos*, Societas Archaeologica Upsaliensis, Uppsala, 1995, p. 168.
6.   *Ibid.* no. 5. p. 205.
7.   DIAMOND J. M. – "The Last People Alive" *Nature*, Vol. 370, 4 Aug 1994, p. 331.
8.   BENT J.T. – *The Ruined Cities of Mashonaland*, Longmans, Green and Co. 1896.
9.   GARLAKE P. S. – "The First Eighty Years of Rock Art Studies, 1890–1970" *Heritage of Zimbabwe, No 12*, The History Society of Zimbabwe, Harare, 1993, p. 2.
10. JONES N. – *The Stone Age in Rhodesia*, Oxford University Press, 1926, p. 107.
11. CRIPPS L. – "Rock Paintings in Southern Rhodesia" *South African Journal of Science*, No. 37, 1941, p. 345.
12. IMPEY S.P. – *Origin of the Bushmen and the Rock Paintings of South Africa*, Juta, Cape Town, 1926.
13. FROBENIUS L. – *Madsimu Dsangara*, 2 vols, Atlantis Verlag, Berlin, 1931.
14. GARLAKE P.G. – "The First Eighty Years of Rock Art Studies, 1890–1970" *Heritage of Zimbabwe*, No. 12, 1993, The History Society of Zimbabwe, p. 15.
15. CLARK J. D., COOKE C.K., GOODALL E., ed. SUMMERS R. – *Prehistoric Rock Art of the Federation of Rhodesia and Nyasaland*, National Publications Trust, Salisbury, 1959.
16. COOKE C.K. – *Rock Art of Southern Africa*, Books of Africa, Cape Town, 1969, p. 149.
17. *Ibid.*, p. 25.
18. KRÜGER J.S. – *Along Edges*, University of South Africa, Pretoria, 1995, p. 161.
19. *Ibid.*, No. 4, p. 133.
20. KINAHAN J. – "Alternative views on the acquisition of livestock by hunter-gatherers in southern Africa." *South African Archaeological Bulletin*, Vol. 51, No. 164, Dec 1996, p. 108.

Chapter 4: The Matopo (pp. 33–44)

Opening Quote: BURKITT M. – *South Africa's Past in Stone and Paint*, Cambridge University Press, 1928, p. 123.
1.   HOLE H.M. – *Lobengula*, Philip Allan & Co, Ltd, London, 1929, p. 65.
2.   TREDGOLD R. (ed) – *The Matopos*, a revised edition of *A Guide to the Matopos* by Dr E.A. Nobbs. The Federal Dept of Printing and Stationery, Salisbury, (Harare) 1956, p. 95.
3.   TWIDALE C.R. – *Granite Landforms*, Elsevier Scientific Publishing Co., Amsterdam, 1982.
4.   WALKER N.J. – *Late Pleistocene and Holocene Hunter-gatherers of the Matopos*, (Doctoral Thesis) Societas Archaeologica Upsaliensis, Uppsala, 1995, p. 21.
5.   STORY R. – "Some plants used by the Bushmen in obtaining food and water" Botanical Survey Memoir No. 3, Dept of Agriculture, Division of Botany, 1958. [Annotated by Miss McCallman]
     WILD H. – *A Southern Rhodesian Botanical Dictionary of Native and English plant names*, Southern Rhodesian Govt Printing and Stationery Dept, 1953
6.   *Ibid.* no. 4, p. 45.
7.   BROADLEY D.G. – "The Herpetofauna of the Matopo" In prep. 1995
8.   NOBBS E.A. – referenced by C.J. Lightfoot, "The History and Natural Resources of the Matopo Hills", *The Zimbabwe Science News*, Vol. 15, No. 11, Nov 1981, p. 213.

Chapter 5: Life Was for Living (pp. 45–61)

Opening Quote: SILBERBAUER G. – *Hunter and Habitat in the Central Kalahari Desert*, Cambridge University Press, 1981, p. xiv.

1. POST L. van der – *Heart of the Hunter*, The Hogarth Press, 1961, p. 120
2. SILBERBAUER G. – *Hunter and Habitat in the Central Kalahri Desert*, Cambridge University Press, 1981, p. 95.
3. *Ibid.*, p. 191.
4. *Ibid.*, p. 195.
5. PFEIFFER J.E. – *The Creative Explosion*, Harper and Row, New York, 1982.
6. LEAKEY R. and LEWIN R. – *Origins Reconsidered*, Little, Brown & Co. London 1992, p. 234.
7. *Ibid.*, no. 2, p. 59.
8. MARSHALL THOMAS E. – *The Harmless People*, Secker & Warburg London, 1959, p. 22.
9. WALKER N.J. – *Late Pleistocene and Holocene Hunter-gatherers of the Matopos*, (Doctoral thesis), Societas Archaeologica Upsaliensis, Uppsala, 1995, p. 54.
10. LEE R.B. – *The Kalahari Hunter Gatherers*, Harvard University Press, Cambridge, Mass., 1976
11. POST L. van der – *The Lost World of the Kalahari*, Hogarth Press, London, 1958, p. 20.
12. *Ibid.*, no. 9, p. 30
13. ELLERT A. – pers. comm.
14. WALKER N.J. – "King of Foods. Marula economics in the Matobos", *African Wildlife*, Vol. 43, No. 6, 1989, p. 281.
14A WANNENBURGH A. JOHNSON P. BANNISTER A. – *The Bushmen*, New Holland, 1979.
15. MOFFAT R. – *Missionary Labours and Scenes in Southern Africa*, John Snow, Paternoster Row, London, 1842, p. 54.
16. KRÜGER J.S. – *Along Edges*, UNISA, Pretoria, 1995, p. 295.
17. *Ibid.*, no. 2. p. 95
18. FRAZER J.G. – *The Golden Bough*, MacMillan and Co, London, 1924, p. 518.

Chapter 6: A Testimony to Timeless, Technical Brilliance (pp. 63–78)

Opening Quote: HUXLEY J. – *The Humanist Frame*, Allen & Unwin, 1961, p. 28.

1. SKOTNES P. – "The visual as a site of meaning", *Contested Images*, ed. T.A. Dowson and D. Lewis Williams, Wits Univ Press, 1994, pg 321.
2. LEAKEY R. and LEWIN R. – *Origins Reconsidered*, Little, Brown and Co. 1992, p. 230.
3. GOMBRICH E.H. – *The Story of Art*, The Companion Book Club, London, 1956, (originally published by Phaidon Press) p. 9.
4. *Ibid.* no 1, p. 321
5. READ H. – *Art Now*, Faber and Faber Ltd, London, 1950, p. 47.
6. GILOT F. – *Life With Picasso*, Penguin, 1965 p. 71.
7. READ H. – *A Concise History of Modern Painting*, Thames and Hudson, London 1974, p. 12.
8. WALKER G. – "Why rock artists turned to animals", *New Scientist*, 22 April 1995, p. 17.
9. HUXLEY J. – *The Humanist Frame*, George Allen and Unwin, London, 1961, p. 34.

Chapter 7: Mind, Myth, Magic or Reality? (pp. 85–128)

Opening Quote: BAHN P.G. – *Cambridge Illustrated History [of] Prehistoric Art*, Cambridge, University Press, 1998, p. 182

1. LEWIS-WILLIAMS D. and DOWSON T.A. – "Aspects of Rock Art Research – A Critical Retrospective." *Contested Images*, ed. Dowson and Lewis-Williams, Wits Univ Press, 1994, p. 206.
2. KATZ R. – *Boiling Energy*, Harvard University Press, Cambridge, Mass., 1982, p. 296.
3. GOMBRICH E.H. – *Art and Illusion*, Phaidon, London, 1994 reprint, p. 92.
4. MENDELOWITZ D.M. – *Drawing*, Holt, Rinehart and Winston, Inc. New York, 1967, p. 6.
5. SILBERBAUER G.B. – *Hunter and Habitat in the central Kalahari Desert*, Cambridge University Press, 1981, p. 57.
6. HALIFAX J. – *Shamanic Voices*, Arkana, [Penguin Group] USA, 1979, p. 104.
7. LASKI M. – *Ecstasy*, The Cresset Press, London, 1961, p. 371.
8. WEATHERALL D. – *Science and the Quiet Art*, Oxford University Press, 1995, p. 178.
9. *Ibid.*, no. 6, p. 3.
10. HUXLEY A. – *The Doors of Perception*, Chatto & Windus, London, 1954, p. 49.
11. BURRETT R. – "Prehistoric drug addiction" Newsletter of The Prehistory Society of Zimbabwe, No. 77, January 1990, pp. 4–7.
12. *Ibid.*, no. 9, p. 15.
13. SAVAGE C.W. – "The Continuity of Perceptual and Cognitive Experiences", *Hallucinations*, ed. Siegel and West, John Wiley and Sons, New York, 1975, p. 262
14. POST L. van der – *Heart of the Hunter*, The Hogarth Press, 1961, p. 236.
15. GARDNER S.W – "Aesthetics", *Philosophy*, ed. by A.C. Grayling, Oxford University Press, 1995, p. 604.
16. MARTIN H. – *The Sheltering Desert*, AD Donker, South Africa, 1996, p. 276.
17. WEBSTER J.H. – *No Finality*, Spiritualist Press Ltd, London, 1951, p. 8.
18. SCHRENK-NOTZING Baron Von – *Phenomena of Materialisation*, Kegan Paul, Trench, Trubner & Co., London, 1923, p. 329.
19. TURNBULL C.M. – *The Forest People*, Book Club Associates, London, 1961, p. 84.
20. POST L. van der – *Heart of the Hunter*, The Hogarth Press, 1961, p. 197.
21. RENFREW C. and BAHN P.G. – *Archaeology*, Thames and Hudson, London, (2nd ed.) 1996, p. 402

... And Now, The Future (p. 127)

Opening Quote: CLOTTES J. – *Rock Art – A universal cultural message*, (translated from the French by Paul Bahn) UNESCO, U.S.A. 1997, p. 23

1. TARUVINGA P. – "The `State of the Art' – Rock Art in Zimbabwe", INORA, No. 16, 1997, p. 27.
2. *Ibid.*, opening quote, p. 15.
Closing Quote: BRONOWSKI J. – *The Ascent of Man*, Futura, London, 1989, p. 33.

Publications Consulted

Ashton E.H. – *The Matopos – Socio-Historical Survey*, Dept of National Parks and Wildlife Management, 1981.

Bahn P.G. and Vertut J. – *Journey Through the Ice Age*, University of California Press, 1997.

Barnard A. – *Hunters and Herders of Southern Africa*, Cambridge University Press, 1992.

Bleek W.H.I. and Lloyd L.C. – *Specimens of Bushmen Folklore*, Struik, Cape Town, 1968. (Originally published by George Allen, 1911)

Broadley D.G. and Blake D.K. – "A check list of the reptiles of the National Parks and the other conservation areas of Zimbabwe Rhodesia." Arnoldia (Rhod.), Vol. 8, No. 35, Sept 8 1979.

Buckle C. – *Landforms in Africa*, Longman Group Ltd, London, 1978.

Brentjes B – *African Rock Art*, (Translated by Anthony Dent), J.M. Dent & Sons, London, 1969.

Carpenter P. and Graham W. – *Art and Ideas*, Mills and Boon, London, 1971.

Cooke C.K. – "Report on Excavations at Pomongwe and Tshangula Caves, Matopo Hills, Southern Rhodesia." *Archaeological Bulletin*, Vol. XVIII, No. 71, Part III, Nov 1963.

Cooke C.K. – "Iron Age Influences in the Rock Art of Southern Africa" *Arnoldia* (Rhod.), Vol. 1, No. 12, June 1964.

Cooke C.K. – "Animals in Southern Rhodesian Rock Art." *Arnoldia* (Rhod.), Vol. 1, No. 13, July 29 1964.

Cooke C.K. – "Human Figures Under Blankets or Skins in Southern Rhodesian Rock Art." *Arnoldia* (Rhod.), Vol. 1, No. 17, Oct 29 1964.

Cooke C.K. – "Mpato Shelter: Sentinel Ranch, Limpopo River, Beitbridge, Rhodesia: Excavation Results." *Arnoldia* (Rhod.) Vol. 4, No. 18, April 14 1969.

Cooke C.K. – "Rock Paintings in Southern Rhodesia." S. Afr. J. Sci., Vol. 37.

Cooke C.K. – "The Cheetah Hunt Paintings", *Arnoldia* (Rhod.), Vol. 6, No. 33, April 9 1974.

Cooke C.K. – "Evidence of Human Migrations from the Rock Art of Southern Rhodesia." International African Institute Reprint From Africa, Vol XXXV, No.3, July 1965, Oxford University Press, 1965.

Cooke C.K. – "Bowmen, Spears and Shields in Southern Rhodesian Rock Art", *Cimbebasia*, No. 10, Windhoek, 1964.

Cooke C.K. and Robinson K.R. – "Excavations at Amadzimba Cave, Located in the Matopo Hills, Southern Rhodesia."

Davis W – One River. Science, Adventure and Hallucinogenics in the Amazon Basin. Simon & Schuster, London, 1997.

Doerner M. – *The Materials of the Artist*, Hart-Davis, MacGibbon, London, 1976.

Garlake P. – *The Painted Caves*, Modus Publications, Harare, 1987.

Henz N.J. – "The Ethno-biology of the !Ko Bushmen: The Anatomical and Physiological Knowledge." *S. Afr. J. Sci.* Feb 1971.

Huffman T.N. – "The Trance Hypothesis and the Rock Art of Zimbabwe." *S. Afr. Archaeological Society Goodwin Series 4*, 1983.

Inskeep R.R. – *The Peopling of Southern Africa*, David Philip, Cape Town, 1978.

Jones N. – *The Prehistory of Southern Rhodesia*, Cambridge University Press, 1949.

Laurie A.P. – *The Painter's Methods and Materials*, Dover Publications, Inc. New York, 1967.

Leakey R. – *The Origin of Humankind*, Weidenfeld & Nicolson, London, 1994.

Levi-Strauss C. – *The Savage Mind*, Weidenfeld & Nicolson, London, 1989.

Lewis-Williams D. – *Reality and Non-Reality in San Rock Art*, Wits University Press, 1988.

Lewis-Williams D. and Dowson T. [ed.] – *Images of Power*, Southern Book Publishers, Johannesburg, 1989.

Lister L.A. – "The Geomorphic Evolution of Zimbabwe Rhodesia." *Transactions of the Geological Society of Southern Africa*, No. 82, 1979.

Livingstone D. – *A Popular Account of Missionary Travels and Researches in South Africa*, John Murray, London, 1875.

Mayer R. – *A Dictionary of Art Terms And Techniques*, Adam and Charles Black, London, 1969.

Morris D. and R. – *Men and Snakes*, Hutchinson & Co., London, 1965.

Penrose R. – *Picasso*, Phaidon Press Ltd, London, 1991.

Phillipson D.W. – *African Archaeology*, Cambridge University Press, 1993.

Rudgley R. – *The Encyclopaedia of Psychoactive Substances*, Little, Brown and Company, London, 1998.

Schapera I. – *The Khoisan Peoples of South Africa*, Routledge & Kegan Paul Ltd, London, 1963.

Smith A.B. – *Pastoralism in Africa*, Wits University Press, Johannesburg, 1992.

Smith R.M. – "Movement patterns and feeding behaviour of Leopard in the Rhodes Matopos National Park, Rhodesia." *Arnoldia* (Rhod.), Vol. 8, No. 13, 18 March 1977.

Stringer C. and McKie R. – *African Exodus*, Pimlico, London, 1997. (Originally published by Jonathan Cape, 1996).

Swift W.N. – "An Outline of the Geology of Southern Rhodesia." *Southern Rhodesia Geological Survey Bulletin*, No. 56.

Tanaka J. – *The San Hunter-gatherers of the Kalahari*, (Translated by D.W. Hughes), University of Tokyo Press, 1980.

Thompson G. – *Travels and Adventures in Southern Africa*, Parts 1, 2, and 3, ed. V.S. Forbes, the Van Riebeck Society, Cape Town, 1967. (Originally published by Henry Colburn, 1827).

White F. – "The Underground Forests of Africa." *Singapore Gardens Bulletin*, 1976.

Wrangham R. and Peterson D. – *Demonic Males, Apes and the Origin of Human Violence*, Bloosbury Publishing PLC, 1997.